Eat Your Way to
Lower
Cholesterol

Eat Your Way to
Lower
Cholesterol

●●●●●●

Recipes to reduce cholesterol by up to 20% in under 3 months

IAN MARBER AND DR LAURA CORR
RECIPES BY DR SARAH SCHENKER

First published in Great Britain in 2014
by Orion Publishing Group Ltd
Orion House, 5 Upper St Martin's Lane
London WC2H 9EA
An Hachette UK Company

10 9 8 7 6 5 4 3 2 1

A CIP catalogue record for this book is available from the British Library.

ISBN: 9781409152071

Design by Smith & Gilmour
Photography by Andrew Hayes-Watkins
Food styling by Justine Pattison
Assistant food styling by Lauren Brignell
Prop styling by Claire Bignell

Printed and bound in Italy

Note: *While every effort has been made to ensure that the information in this
book is correct, it should not be substituted for medical advice. The recipes in
this book should be used in combination with a healthy lifestyle. If you are
concerned about any aspect of your health, speak to your GP. People under
medical supervision should not come off their medication without speaking
to their health professional.*

www.orionbooks.co.uk

Contents

Preface

The chances are, if you are reading this book, you have been to your GP, had a blood test and been told you have to reduce your cholesterol. If it's not you, it might be someone you know – around 60 per cent of the British population have blood cholesterol levels that are a cause for concern.

Most people are aware that there is a strong link between high cholesterol and the risk of heart disease. And if you've been told to get your levels down, it's to reduce that risk. So what now?

Firstly, it is important to realise that numbers are not everything. I know this seems an odd thing to say in a book about lowering your cholesterol, but the risk of heart disease also depends on genetic predisposition, smoking cigarettes, diabetes, high blood pressure, lack of exercise and obesity, among other things. In fact, the majority of those who suffer a heart attack have cholesterol levels that are still considered 'normal'. Even so, cholesterol is a fundamental part of the problem, and tackling it will help everyone who is worried.

If your doctor thinks your particular risk is very high and has recommended medication in the form of statins you should try to follow that advice. Statins can rapidly lower harmful types of cholesterol by an impressive 60 per cent or more, and they also have other roles in preventing heart disease.

But whether or not drug treatment is needed, lifestyle is fundamentally important – and a central part of lowering risk comes down to diet. As a cardiologist, I am all too aware that much advice on how to lower cholesterol is vague or confusing, often focusing on what you can't eat. But recently, large-scale studies have indicated that it's the foods you should be eating that are just as important as those you shouldn't. Adding certain foods to your diet can actually lower cholesterol and reduce the risk of heart disease and strokes.

New evidence has shown a reduction in LDL cholesterol by as much as 20 per cent in three months when a combination of these foods was taken with a healthy diet. And the more often the foods were eaten, the greater the benefit. Ian Marber and I have looked at the most up-to-date international research and identified six foods for which there is the best evidence. With the help of dietician Dr Sarah Schenker, we have included these foods in healthy, easy-to-prepare and delicious recipes. Our hope is that everyone will enjoy them – whether they need help with their heart or not.

Dr Laura Corr
Consultant Cardiologist
Guy's and St Thomas' Hospitals

Introduction

We all know a bit about food and health. Whether from old wives' tales, messages from our school days or things we've seen in television adverts, these pieces of information lodge in our brain and influence us. If you feel a cold coming on then you might eat an orange as it's a source of vitamin C. Or you might eat a banana for muscle cramp just like we see tennis professionals doing mid-match. Interestingly, many bits of information that we think of as fact have been disproven over the years. If you think about cholesterol and diet, there are several elements that might form part of our default opinion. Avoiding eggs, shellfish, red meat, milk or cheese for instance.

The good news is that the science has moved on. Most people, about two-thirds of the population, can eat an egg every day, enjoy some red meat and eat dairy products without worrying about cholesterol. The important point to note is that cholesterol in the food we eat does not have a powerful effect on raising cholesterol levels in the blood. The body generally compensates. But there is now strong evidence that protection from heart disease and strokes comes just as much from foods we should be including in our diets, as those we should be avoiding. The latest research shows that eating specific foods can not only lower cholesterol levels but also have wider-ranging benefits for heart health.

What is cholesterol anyway?

Most people think of cholesterol simply as a bad thing but it's not. In fact, this fatty, waxy substance is essential for life. It is in the wall of all the cells in the body, insulates our nerve fibres and is also needed to make sex and stress hormones. Most cholesterol in the blood is made by our own body, particularly by the liver, which can in fact make cholesterol from almost any food you eat. The liver adjusts the amount it makes in response to the amount of cholesterol circulating in the blood. This is why, for most people, if you eat cholesterol-containing foods like eggs or shellfish your blood cholesterol doesn't change – the liver simply makes less.

As well as releasing cholesterol directly into the blood, the liver uses some cholesterol to make bile. Bile is a digestive fluid secreted into the gut that helps us absorb fat from the food we eat. Bile cholesterol is either reabsorbed and recycled by the liver, or is passed out as waste. This is the main way that cholesterol is eliminated from the blood.

We all know that oil and water don't mix, and because cholesterol is a type of fat, and blood is mostly water, these two wouldn't get along without an important addition. In order for the cholesterol to be transported easily in the bloodstream, the liver coats it in proteins. The resulting tiny balls of fat are known as lipoproteins, and it is these we are usually referring to when we talk about cholesterol.

There are two main types of lipoprotein that are relevant to us: **low-density lipoprotein** (LDL) and **high-density lipoprotein** (HDL). This is why, when you have a blood test to check your cholesterol levels, your GP might give you more than one number.

LDL

- The main function of LDL is to carry cholesterol to the cells of the body where it is needed.
- If there is more than is needed by the body's cells, LDL can build up in spots in the artery walls – a process called atherosclerosis.
- Once this starts, the LDL can undergo a chemical change called oxidation – a process akin to butter going rancid – causing further damage to the artery walls and raising the risk of heart disease.

HDL

- The main function of HDL is to mop up the excess LDL cholesterol and take it away from the cells and artery walls to the liver, where it is either broken down or excreted.
- The more HDL we have, the better. A person can have high overall cholesterol levels but if much of it is HDL, then they probably won't be told to get their levels down.

How does eating more of certain foods reduce cholesterol?

Making adjustments to your diet can reduce overall cholesterol in various ways:

1 Certain foods, such as fibre-rich beans and pulses or oats, stop cholesterol from being absorbed into the blood circulation.

2 There is also evidence that certain types of fibre actually reduce the amount of cholesterol manufactured by the liver.

3 In addition, there are some foods, including nuts, olive and rapeseed oils, that may stop LDL from causing damage.

These three key aspects are represented in the six foods outlined in the following pages. By eating all of these foods every day as part of a balanced diet, you could lower your cholesterol levels significantly within three months.

We will look at each of the six foods individually, in detail, so that you can see exactly how each element works and how much of each food you would have to eat to achieve the required effective 'cholesterol-lowering' dose.

And then on to the best part – the tempting recipes and snack suggestions that will make it easy for you to include these 'healthful' foods into your diet every day. The recipes cover every occasion, from fuss-free lunches to hearty feasts, as well as clever takes on classic dishes. Each recipe has a helpful key showing you which of the six foods are included and at what dose (see How to use this book, page 21).

There is also a 14-day menu planner that can be followed to ensure that you get all six foods, but can also be used if you prefer to focus on, say, just three of the foods (see pages 182–185).

Even if your LDL doesn't come down there will be other important benefits from these six foods to help protect you from heart disease. To find out more, turn to the section, Frequently asked questions, on page 178.

If you adopt just a few, or don't manage all six every day then you can still reap significant benefits. We hope our diet will make it as pleasurable as possible to take positive steps towards being in control of your health.

How do we know the diet works?

The six foods on pages 10–16 have been selected because they have a proven effect on blood cholesterol.

In each case the findings of the most significant studies into each food are outlined, alongside an idea about how each might impact on cholesterol.

Also mentioned is a 'daily dose' – how much you would have to eat of each food every day and for how long, before you saw an improvement.

One serving of each recipe contains either a full or a half dose of one or more of the foods. Refer to the meal planners on pages 182–185 to try and achieve a dose of all six foods or more every day. Or simply focus on one or two – either way you will still see a reduction. You may notice that the percentage reduction of each food added together would be greater than the 20 per cent mentioned on the cover.

That is because most of the studies examined the effects of one or two of these foods at a time and the effect of all six foods eaten in combination incorporated into a normal healthy diet has not been widely examined yet.

However, several small studies from the University of Toronto did look at the combination (minus olive oil), within the confines of a strictly controlled vegetarian diet in a lab setting, and found a reduction in LDL ('bad') cholesterol of around 30 per cent. When these researchers followed up participants for a year in the 'real world' outside the lab, the reduction in LDL averaged at 13 per cent, with a drop of over 20 per cent seen in those who ate more of the recommended foods.

As mentioned previously, numbers are not everything. In the case of nuts and oils, we don't give a percentage reduction – although there are various small studies that do show they have this effect. However, in the case of these two foods, the most important thing is that they change the type of cholesterol in circulation to make it either less damaging, or beneficial, which is equally important to heart health.

Introducing the six foods

1. Fibre

Fibre is, essentially, plant matter that is indigestible (to humans, at least). There are various kinds – cellulose, inulin, pectin and others – found in different combinations in various foods. Oats and grains (and therefore certain types of bread) are the richest sources of fibre, but wholemeal bread, bran, cereals, beans, pulses, nuts, seeds, vegetables and fruit all contain fibre too.

If anything is a superfood this is it: fibre aids digestion, helping food move through the intestines, and can help protect against bowel cancer and other diseases. Some fibres are insoluble and stay intact, but absorb water and become bulky. Others are soluble – they break down into a gel when mixed with water. All fibre-giving foods contain both soluble and insoluble fibres, but it is soluble fibre in particular that may help lower cholesterol.

How it works

Countless studies have proven that soluble fibre lowers cholesterol but, surprisingly, the exact way in which it works is still unknown. Nevertheless three processes are important.

Firstly, soluble fibre can bind to bile, which means that as the fibre passes through the digestive tract the bile goes as a passenger with it. As a result, more bile is lost as waste in the presence of soluble fibre, instead of being reabsorbed by the liver. This means the liver has to make more bile, and it takes cholesterol out of the bloodstream to do this.

Secondly, soluble fibre helps some of the fats in food pass through the body without being taken up. Though only a quarter of cholesterol comes directly from food

FIBRE SUGGESTIONS

- Eat fruit whole rather than in juice or smoothies. There is almost 5g of fibre in a whole orange, yet less than 2g in a serving of orange juice.
- Try to eat the skin of fruit and vegetables for maximum fibre. Did you know that kiwi skin is edible and delicious? Skin-on, they provide almost 3g of fibre – and by not peeling, you preserve more of the vitamin C content as well.
- Choose seeded wholemeal or other grain-based varieties of bread. Opt for brown or wholemeal rice and pasta rather than white.
- Beans and pulses are the richest source of fibres – half a tin of baked beans provides 9g. When buying tinned beans, choose unsalted, no added sugar varieties.
- Use butter beans in place of potato as a thickener and flavour-enhancer in homemade soups.
- If you are making a pâté or spread add a heaped teaspoon of oats or any savoury grain into the mix providing you with an extra boost of fibre.
- Sprinkle a generous tablespoon of mixed seeds (such as sunflower, pumpkin, sesame) over salads to add 1–2g of fibre.

fat, limiting it can't hurt. The gel-like soluble fibre forms a barrier between the food fat and the gut wall, slowing or preventing it from being broken down by bile and being absorbed.

Finally, fibre can be fermented by naturally occurring bacteria in the gut, making substances that reduce the ability of the liver to make cholesterol.

Daily dose

Current government advice is that we should consume 18g of fibre daily – but this really isn't enough. Research suggests that diets with 20g or more of fibre a day are associated with lower cholesterol levels. It's not easy to get this entire dose all in one 'hit', and might even cause some digestive discomfort if you tried this. In general we recommend that at least 9g of fibre should come from oats (see page 15), leaving a minimum of 11g to come from other sources, such as beans and pulses, vegetables, fruit – whole, not juice – and other wholegrains. Studies suggest that this combination, eaten daily for three months may result in a cholesterol reduction of 12 per cent. As we have said, all fibre-containing foods are made up of both insoluble and soluble types, and our recipes provide a balanced amount of both.

2. Healthy oils

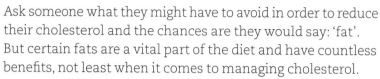

Ask someone what they might have to avoid in order to reduce their cholesterol and the chances are they would say: 'fat'. But certain fats are a vital part of the diet and have countless benefits, not least when it comes to managing cholesterol.

Broadly speaking, there are two types of fat: saturated and unsaturated. Many foods contain both in differing amounts – typically, animal fat and dairy products are higher in saturated fat (although these both contain unsaturated fats too). However, it's unsaturated fat we are particularly interested in – and this is found in abundance in olive and rapeseed oil. Ideally the oil you use should be of good quality – and eaten cold or warm. The word 'virgin' in olive oil production is used when the oil has been extracted by mechanical means only and no chemicals or heat have been used. Consequently, the more virgin the oil, the higher the concentration of those beneficial compounds.

How it works

Although we know that these oils protect against cardio-vascular disease, they may not actively lower LDL levels. But they can raise 'good' HDL levels relative to your total cholesterol. As we have said, the more HDL cholesterol you have, the better. The oils also contain compounds called phenolic acid and vitamin E, both of which can offer some protection from the damage caused by LDL oxidation (see page 8). Avoid heating these oils at high temperatures as this causes them to smoke, making them ineffective. Instead, pour the oils on to hot food. Oils should be stored in the fridge or in a cool place and protected from direct sunlight.

Daily dose

Studies show that we should have at least 25ml virgin or extra virgin olive oil a day. That's no less than two tablespoons. As well as using our recipes, you can drizzle oil over salads, steamed vegetables or use in place of butter on granary bread.

3. Soya

● ● ● ● ● ●

Once considered rather exotic, soya products are becoming increasingly familiar. Soya milk, tofu – which is made from soya milk – soya beans (often called edamame), yoghurt, ice cream and cheese made from soya milk are all available from most supermarkets. Another excellent soya option is soya mince. We use this a fair bit in the recipes that follow and it is also available at all good supermarkets or healthfood stores.

While soya has cholesterol-reducing properties, it is also naturally low in saturated fat and a great source of protein. As a result, replacing foods that you might normally eat with this low-fat alternative is another way that soya can help reduce cholesterol. It also contains unsaturated fats that can play a role, in the same way olive and rapeseed oil do (see opposite page on healthy oils).

How it works

The exact mechanism isn't yet fully understood, but it is likely that isoflavones – organic compounds found in soya – may reduce the amount of LDL made by the body. Research suggests that the reduction of cholesterol attributable to eating soya is modest but it's a very useful food when combined with our other foods.

Daily dose

A recent analysis of over 40 studies by the University of Kentucky concluded that 30g of soya products eaten daily might reduce cholesterol by 1 per cent. That's half a litre of soya milk and a soya yoghurt daily, or 30g tofu. The studies ranged in length from 4 to 18 weeks, so you should start to see a difference after a month, but it could take longer.

SOYA SUGGESTIONS

● ● ● ● ● ●

- Add soya milk to your daily tea and coffee. Opt for the unsweetened varieties. Also try soya drinks, which are a mixture of fruit juices and soya milk.
- Add some cubed tofu to a soup, stir-fry or mix into a salad, or use some silken tofu, which is very soft and gives a smooth and velvety texture if blended into a homemade smoothie along with a little juice, fresh fruit and soya milk.
- Add green soya beans (edamame) to risottos, salads and pasta dishes – they are widely available frozen and can be defrosted quickly, much like frozen peas.
- Soy sauce is not recommended as it is mostly water, and can be overly salty.
- Try using soya cheeses. They are available in many varieties – from Cheddar to mozzarella – and are an excellent way to incorporate soya into meals.

4. Nuts

Almonds, Brazils, hazelnuts, macadamias, pecans, pistachios and walnuts are brilliantly versatile and have a beneficial effect on cholesterol. Those conscious of their waistlines might think they need to avoid them, as they are quite calorific, but a recent study that looked at the benefits of a 'Mediterranean' diet found that eating around 30g – that's a good-sized handful – of nuts per day as part of that diet did not lead to weight gain. This may seem counter-intuitive, but due to the combination of fibre, fat and protein, which satisfies appetite, less is eaten overall. Recent research suggests that when raw nuts are eaten not all the calories are actually absorbed.

How it works

Nuts and seeds are rich in fibre and unsaturated fats – the benefits of which have already been explained – but they are also sources of vitamin E and phenolic acid, much like olive and rapeseed oil. Like those, the most authoritative research shows they might not actively reduce overall cholesterol, but boost levels of HDL instead, and they may make LDL less damaging. There have been trials that looked at the effect of nuts alone, and they found participants who ate on average more than twice our dose (67g) experienced a drop in overall cholesterol of 5 per cent.

Daily dose

As in the study mentioned above, about 30g of nuts a day should suffice. Though nuts are of course all different, and 30g equates to, for instance, about 20 almonds, 10 Brazil nuts or 15 cashews. This is roughly the dose we have used in our recipes.

NUT SUGGESTIONS

- Nuts should be unsalted, as excess sodium in the diet may contribute to high blood pressure, and should be without added sugar, as sugars might actually raise cholesterol.
- Uncooked nuts are best, as excess heat can degrade the quality of their fat. If you do heat them, make sure not to burn them.
- Store in a cool place in an airtight jar to keep them fresh for longer.
- Try adding a couple of vanilla pods to a jar full of nuts, giving it a shake every now and again. Vanilla-scented nuts put a zing in any breakfast, whether mixed with yoghurt, crumbled over fruit salad or stirred into porridge.

5. Oats (and other beta-glucan foods)

● ● ● ● ● ●

When it comes to 'oats' most people instantly think of porridge. Although it's very versatile, there are many other ways to enjoy your dose of oats. Try Bircher muesli, oatcakes and other clever ways to sneak oats into food, such as in coatings for fish.

Oats contain a specific soluble fibre called beta-glucan, also found in lesser amounts in barley, some yeasts and algae as well as some exotic mushrooms, such as shiitake and oyster. It is this compound that has the cholesterol-lowering effect.

How it works

Beta-glucan binds to cholesterol in the intestines preventing it from being absorbed into the blood. It also offers some protection against the oxidation of LDL. A 2011 study rounded up evidence from 126 clinical studies and confirmed that total cholesterol and LDL were both reduced after the consumption of beta-glucan and that HDL levels rose.

Daily dose

The studies show just 3g of beta-glucan from oat or barley daily is sufficient to reduce blood cholesterol by 5–10 per cent. The benefits should be measurable after about six weeks but may take longer in some cases.

The beta-glucan content of oats is between 2 and 8 per cent of the dry weight. That is, 100g of oats would supply 2–8g of beta-glucan. Whether the oats are relatively high or low in beta-glucan depends upon two factors. There is the simple variation between crops – some oats just have more, some have less – but beta-glucan content is also affected by how the oats are processed. Rougher oats tend to contain more beta-glucan than the processed instant varieties (which may also contain added sugar). You have no control over the crop itself, but you can favour less processed oats.

One oatcake will give you, on average, around 1g of beta glucan. A small bowl of porridge serves up over 3g, and a slice of oat bread (which is often a mixture of wheat and oats) should give you 0.5g per slice. In our recipes, approximately 90g of oats counts as a whole dose.

6. Smart foods

Research also shows that
there is little further benefit
from having more than 2.5g
of sterols a day, so two
stanol shots won't be more
effective than one. Sterols
can be taken 'naturally'.
Broccoli has one of the
highest concentrations of
sterols found in vegetables,
but to get 2g you would
have to eat 4kg in one go.

Unless you have been living under a rock for the past decade,
you'll be at least aware of the yoghurt shots, margarine-like
spreads and other fortified foods that claim to 'actively lower
your cholesterol'.

These foods – the best-known brands are Flora pro-activ
and Benecol – contain stanols and sterols, two very similar
naturally occurring chemical compounds found in plant cell
walls that have a structure similar to cholesterol. In the 1980s
food technologists found a way to isolate these compounds
from plants, which allowed them to be added to other foods.

How they work

The exact mechanism isn't fully clear, but we do know that
plant sterols and stanols have a chemical structure similar to
cholesterol. Because of this, it is believed that they can 'fool'
the gut. They displace the cholesterol found in bile or in the
food we eat and stop it from being absorbed in the intestine.
This leads to a reduction of the amount of cholesterol that
ends up in the blood. There is also evidence that sterols and
stanols can interfere with the regulation of cholesterol levels
by the liver. Very little of the sterols and stanols get absorbed.

Daily dose

Studies suggest 2g of sterols with the largest meal may
provide up to a 15 per cent reduction in cholesterol after three
months. Importantly, less than 2g offers little benefit. It is
harder to track how much you're getting if you try to divvy
up the 2g across smaller amounts over the course of the day:
a swash of enriched spread followed by a splash of fortified
milk. The most practical way to get 2g is by having a sugar-free
stanol shot drink with the largest meal of the day (when we
produce the most digestive juices, and therefore most
cholesterol). For most of us that means with or immediately
after dinner. However, some of our recipes cleverly
incorporate smart foods, providing a dose in themselves.

Mythbusting

There are a number of myths or 'untruths' when it comes to cholesterol. Certain foods are singled out as being 'high in cholesterol' – a phrase that is often wrong and always misleading. Dairy products, red meat, eggs and shellfish are commonly believed to be 'no go' areas. They may have associated problems – though on some the jury is out – but there are ways that you can still include these foods in your diet. As ever, moderation is the key.

Dairy

Dairy foods are typically high in saturated fats, which are linked to high cholesterol, and yet we say that you can drink milk and eat some cheese. Confused?

In fact recent research shows that people who have a higher intake of milk and cheese do not necessarily have higher rates of heart disease. This may be because saturated fat is an umbrella term for many different compounds and not all are classed as unhealthy.

As mentioned, part of eating to improve cholesterol involves plenty of fat in the form of healthy oils such as olive and rapeseed. That is because they contain unsaturated fats that have beneficial effects. Is it possible that saturated fat is not the villain it was once thought to be? There is a huge amount of controversy about this, and there is actually very little robust data on the subject of how much saturated fat we can eat – whether we have high cholesterol or not. For now it may be prudent to follow the British Dietetics Association advice that a balanced diet includes no more than 20g of saturated fat per day for women and 30g for men. And that should be a third of total fat intake. It's not lavish – less than 100g of hard cheese a day (about a matchbox size piece) – but that's certainly not the penance you might have thought it to be. Eaten in moderation like this, there is little or no evidence that dairy causes harm to heart health.

The opposite may be true however. It appears that cutting saturated fat and replacing it with refined carbohydrates – like added sugar in some low-fat dairy products for instance may lower 'good' HDL and increase heart disease risk.

Red meat

Steak lovers can breathe a sigh of relief. Contrary to popular belief red meat isn't outlawed for those trying to reduce their cholesterol. Lamb, beef and pork do contain saturated fats, but then for that matter so does chicken, which is generally considered a low-fat option. However, they also contain the healthier unsaturated fats; pork fat, for instance, is 60 per cent unsaturated. There isn't much data on how much red meat we can eat, but it can be part of your 20g saturated fat per day for women and 30g for men.

If you are going to enjoy red meat, try and restrict it to just once or twice a week and try to choose the leaner cuts. UK Government labelling guidelines state that for beef to be labelled as 'lean' it must contain less than 4.5g saturated fat per 100g.

Eggs

It is surprising how many people still believe that eggs are a key food to avoid if you are watching your cholesterol. For those egg-lovers out there, the good news is that eggs are indeed an acceptable food choice in a low-cholesterol diet. In fact, most people can eat one or two several times a week without affecting their cholesterol levels.

It was in the 1960s that the link was first made between eggs and cholesterol, but the facts were oversimplified and widely misunderstood. As we mentioned before, the liver produces less of its own cholesterol if we eat more – so the majority of people will find their levels don't change when they eat eggs.

But, it must be noted that about 30 per cent of the population are what we call 'hyper-responders': their liver doesn't react as effectively, meaning that cholesterol-containing foods like eggs will push up blood levels. However, even amongst them, there is some evidence that this cholesterol isn't as damaging as HDL increases too. While an egg yolk does contain around 4.5g of fat, most of this is unsaturated

A FEW WORDS ABOUT . . . A BALANCED DIET

Lowering your cholesterol through diet is more about incorporating the right foods rather than just cutting out foods. For best results, however, you will need to stick to a diet that is, overall, balanced. But just what does that mean?

In a nutshell, this means a balance of the food groups, and a balance of protein, fibre, nutrients, carbohydrate and fat. A varied diet. One that includes regular burgers, pizzas and pasties or is overflowing in chips, white bread and pasta, fizzy sugared drinks, biscuits, cakes and sweets is not a balanced one. These foods should be eaten in moderation, if at all.

Likewise, processed meats – sausages, bacon, salami and the like – should only be used sparingly as they have been linked to heart disease. The vast majority of meat you eat should be fresh, unprocessed, organic or at least free-range.

Junk foods may also contain trans-fats, the one thing that is off-limits in our cholesterol-lowering diet. These are fats that have been chemically altered in a lab, and are used in pre-prepared meals and foods. They have no health benefits, and may directly increase cholesterol levels in the blood. What's more your intake of sugar and other refined carbohydrates will be too high, and recent studies suggest that this might have a similar effect on cholesterol as trans-fats.

If you follow our meal planners, your diet will be balanced – high in fresh produce, lean protein, beans, wholegrains, fibre and good fats. But if you wish to go it alone and simply incorporate the six foods into your own recipes and daily routine, as long as you follow the same principles, then that's fine.

A balanced diet doesn't exclude the occasional takeaway or the like, but the more foods you eat that fall into the 'good' category, the better. Not just for cholesterol, but for all aspects of your health.

and is therefore not as bad for you as you might think. If your numbers are not coming down on your diet, you may be a hyper-responder. In this case, try the egg-free recipes.

Shellfish

The ban on prawns is another misconception still commonly held when it comes to cholesterol. Oysters, mussels, squid and shrimp all contain varying amounts of dietary cholesterol. But, as with eggs, we now know for most of us that this has little impact on the amount in our blood. We have found no hard evidence to suggest that shellfish should be avoided. In fact there is strong evidence to support a regular intake of fish – around three times a week – to protect the heart. This not only includes fresh fish but smoked fish and tinned oily fish such as tuna, mackerel and salmon. Shellfish can be taken as part of this too.

Sugar

We know from large studies that people who have high intakes of sugar are more likely to be obese and to have lower levels of 'good' HDL. There isn't a hard and fast figure for how much you can eat, and research is still needed. What is clear is that it's the type of sugar that matters – refined sugars including table sugar, powdered fruit sugars, fruit juices, honey and syrup may have the worst effects, whereas naturally occurring sugars, such as those found in fruit, are fine as the fibre also found in these foods helps slow the speed at which the sugar is absorbed.

There is a very small amount of sugar in our recipes, and even then only when the recipe really calls for it. Including refined sugar in your diet, perhaps in tea and coffee, or sprinkled on cereals and porridge, could undo some of the benefits of our six foods. The solution is to enjoy the food without the sugar and only eat desserts or sweet treats very occasionally. The sweet treats included in this book are low in sugar but even so, they should only be enjoyed once or twice a week. We think that's a small price to pay for such a worthwhile benefit. On a related note, if you do want a couple of squares of chocolate, after dinner for example, then choose one that has at least 70 per cent cocoa solids, as this will be lower in sugar.

How to use this book

Each recipe includes coloured dots that show how many of the six foods it incorporates. A full dot represents one effective dose of that particular food per serving, per day. Many recipes will include half dots or more than one dot and the aim is for you to mix and match to achieve all six dots each day. To the right is a helpful colour code for the dots. We have devised a 14-day meal planner to help you achieve your daily dose, see pages 182–185.

SIX FOODS KEY

- Fibre
- Healthy oils
- Soya
- Nuts
- Oats
- Smart foods

Feta and pomegranate couscous with almonds

SERVES 2

50g frozen edamame
(green soya beans)
100g couscous
200ml hot chicken
or vegetable stock
40g flaked almonds
1 pomegranate or 100g
pomegranate seeds
½ yellow pepper,
deseeded and diced
½ apple, peeled and grated
10 cherry tomatoes, halved
10 black olives, pitted
and halved
50g feta-style soya cheese,
diced
2 tbsp olive oil
Handful flat-leaf parsley,
chopped
Freshly ground black pepper

If you haven't tried cheese made with soya then give this recipe a go – it's delicious. Soya cheese is available from healthfood stores or online. Couscous is easy to prepare and is a wonderful base for salads as it really soaks up the flavours of other ingredients.

Place the frozen edamame in a pan of water and bring to the boil. Simmer for 1–2 minutes and then drain well.

Put the couscous into a bowl and pour over the hot stock. Cover with cling film and then leave for 5 minutes until the couscous has swelled and absorbed all of the stock. Fluff up with a fork to separate the grains.

Put the flaked almonds in a dry frying pan and toast over a medium-high heat until golden brown. Tip out and allow to cool.

If using whole pomegranate, cut it in half and, holding each half over the bowl of couscous, firmly tap the skin with a rolling pin to extract the seeds. Add all the remaining ingredients, except the parsley, and toss gently together. Season with black pepper to taste. Serve with the chopped parsley scattered over the top.

58   Fuss-free lunches

BREAKFAST AND BRUNCH

Yoghurt with almonds, honey and watermelon

SERVES 1

30g flaked almonds
150g unsweetened soya
 yoghurt
1 passion fruit
1–2 tsp honey
1 slice watermelon

This is a delicious way to jazz up plain yoghurt for breakfast, although it would also work well as a healthy dessert. Take care when toasting almonds as they burn easily.

Toast the flaked almonds in a dry frying pan over a low heat for a few minutes, until they turn golden. Remove from the pan and allow to cool.

Tip the yoghurt into a bowl and stir in the almonds. Cut the passion fruit in half, scoop out the seeds and stir them into the yoghurt. Add the honey according to taste and serve with a large slice of watermelon on the side.

Perfect granola

SERVES 8-10

350g jumbo oats
50g oat bran
50g sesame seeds
50g sunflower seeds
50g unskinned almonds,
    roughly chopped
50g desiccated coconut
5 tbsp rapeseed oil

Shop-bought granola can be surprisingly high in sugar so it's always preferable to make your own – that way you know exactly what you are putting in. Enjoy as a breakfast cereal with unsweetened soya milk or as a crunchy topping on yoghurt or mixed berries.

Preheat the oven to 180°C/350°F/Gas mark 4. Mix all the ingredients together in a large bowl until well combined.

Tip the mixture out on to two baking trays and spread evenly. Bake in the oven for 15–20 minutes until golden brown and crisp, stirring every 5–10 minutes. Tip out on to a large tray to cool. Store in an airtight container for up to 3 weeks.

Oat berry smoothie

SERVES 1

1 small banana
50g mixed berries
    (e.g. blueberries,
    raspberries or hulled
    strawberries)
200ml unsweetened
    soya milk
40g fine oatmeal
1 stanol shot

The oats add a lovely texture, making this a satisfying and filling smoothie to enjoy for breakfast or as a pick-me-up drink in the afternoon.

Put the banana, berries and soya milk into a blender and whizz until smooth. Stir in the oatmeal and pour into a container or flask.

Leave to chill in the fridge for at least 1 hour or overnight (this is perfect to make the night before).

Blueberry instant porridge with soya milk

SERVES 1

30g sugar-free instant
  porridge oats
200ml unsweetened
  soya milk
40g blueberries
25g flaked almonds

Porridge is a fantastic, cholesterol-lowering way to start the day. This creamy version, made with unsweetened soya milk, has added blueberries for extra flavour.

Put the oats into a saucepan and pour in the milk. Bring to the boil and simmer for 2–3 minutes, stirring all the time to make sure the porridge doesn't stick to the pan.

Place the blueberries in a bowl and lightly crush with the back of a spoon. Add them to the porridge and swirl together. Serve sprinkled with the flaked almonds.

Almond butter
on toasted muffin

SERVES 1

250g whole almonds,
  unskinned
1 tbsp clear honey,
  such as wildflower
1 wholemeal English muffin
1 red apple, cored and sliced

Making your own almond butter is a great way to introduce one of the six cholesterol-lowering foods into your diet. We've added a little honey for sweetness but it tastes just as good without.

Preheat the oven to 190°C/375°F/Gas mark 5.

Spread the almonds out on a baking tray and bake in the oven for 10 minutes. Remove and allow to cool.

Put into a food processor and whizz for 10–15 minutes until smooth, stopping every so often to scrape the sides down. Transfer to a bowl and stir in the honey. This recipe makes about 8 tablespoons of the nut butter but it will keep in the fridge for up to 3 weeks in an airtight container.

Split and toast the muffin. Meanwhile cut the apple in half, remove the core and cut each half into thin slices. When the muffin is toasted, spread generously with a tablespoon or so of the almond butter and top with apple slices.

French toast with plums

SERVES 2

6 plums, halved and stoned
5 tbsp orange juice
2 slices seeded wholemeal
    bread
2 eggs
1 tbsp milk
2 tbsp rapeseed oil
Pinch ground cinnamon

French toast, or eggy bread, has long been a breakfast favourite – it's easy and quick to make and can be eaten on its own or as part of a more substantial breakfast. This healthy alternative, served with cooked plums, uses seeded wholemeal bread for that extra hit of fibre.

Place the plum halves in a small pan and add the orange juice. Place over a low heat and cook for about 8 minutes, until the plums are soft and sticky but still retain their shape. Set aside.

Cut the bread slices in half diagonally. Crack the eggs into a bowl, add the milk and beat together with a fork.

Heat the oil in a large frying pan. Dip a piece of bread into the egg and milk mixture, making sure it is thoroughly coated, and then put it straight into the hot pan. Cook for 2–3 minutes over a medium heat until golden and then turn over and cook for another 2–3 minutes. Repeat with the other slices.

Sprinkle with the cinnamon and serve with the cooked plums.

Oat pancakes with bananas

SERVES 4

180g oats
700ml unsweetened
    soya milk
3 eggs, beaten
100g plain flour
2 tsp baking powder
Pinch salt
1 tbsp rapeseed oil,
    plus extra for oiling
60g pecan nuts, chopped
2 bananas, sliced

These pancakes are very easy to make and the pecans add a lovely texture.

Put the oats into a large bowl and add the soya milk. Cover and refrigerate overnight to let the oats soak in the milk.

Remove the oats from the fridge and whisk in the eggs, flour, baking powder, salt and oil until you have a thick, smooth batter. Stir through the chopped pecan nuts.

Heat a large frying pan to medium-high heat. Lightly oil the pan and drop large spoonfuls of the pancake batter on to the pan to the desired size, usually about 12–15cm in diameter. After about 2–3 minutes air bubbles should start to appear in the surface of the pancakes. Use a spatula to flip them over and cook for a further 2 minutes until golden. Keep the cooked pancakes warm while you cook the rest.

Serve the pancakes with sliced banana.

Oats three ways

Oats are a fabulous way to start the day and these three recipes show that there is more to oats than just plain porridge. All these can be prepared the night before, giving you that little bit of extra time in the morning.

1 Bircher with rhubarb and ginger compote

SERVES 1

250g rhubarb, trimmed
    and cut into 3cm chunks
Zest and juice of 1 orange
2cm piece fresh ginger,
    peeled and finely chopped
1 tbsp honey
150g unsweetened
    soya yoghurt
45g oats

The sharpness of rhubarb is countered by the sweet honey in this recipe, while the oats add a lovely nutty flavour and texture. If you have any leftover compote, it will keep in the fridge for 2–3 days and is perfect on top of porridge.

Preheat the oven to 180°C/350°F/Gas mark 4.

Put the rhubarb, orange zest and juice and fresh ginger in an ovenproof dish and drizzle with the honey. Cook in the oven, uncovered, for 30–40 minutes. Allow to cool and then transfer to an airtight container.

Put the yoghurt in a bowl and stir in the oats. Chill in the fridge for at least 1 hour (overnight is preferable). When ready to eat, top with rhubarb compote.

2 Apple juice bircher with yoghurt, cinnamon and walnuts

SERVES 1

45g oats
1 tbsp raisins
100ml apple juice
150g unsweetened
    natural soya yoghurt
Pinch ground cinnamon
30g walnuts

Getting creative with nuts and oats and using them as a topping is an easy way to achieve your daily dose. Walnuts are particularly beneficial as they contain decent levels of omega-3, essential for heart health.

Place the oats and raisins in a bowl and pour over the apple juice. Leave to chill in the fridge for at least 1 hour, preferably overnight.

When ready to eat, top with the yoghurt and sprinkle over the cinnamon and walnuts.

3 Apple juice bircher with mango and hazelnut crunch

SERVES 1

45g oats
100ml apple juice
½ mango
30g unskinned hazelnuts,
    roughly chopped

Soaking oats in apple juice makes them soft and deliciously chewy, while the mango and hazelnut crunch adds sweetness and texture.

Place the oats in a bowl and pour over the apple juice. Leave to chill in the fridge for at least 1 hour, preferably overnight.

Peel and slice the mango into thin strips. Serve on top of the oats along with a sprinkle of chopped hazelnuts.

Oat beetroot muffins

MAKES 12

150g wholemeal flour
150g oats
1½ tsp baking powder
½ tsp baking soda
Pinch salt
1 tsp ground cinnamon
1 tsp mixed spice
2 medium beetroots,
    scrubbed and
    coarsely grated
50g raisins
50g chopped walnuts
1 over-ripe banana
100ml rapeseed oil
2 tbsp honey
2 eggs, beaten
250ml unsweetened
    soya milk

A healthy and filling alternative breakfast. Beetroot is a surprisingly good addition to cakes and muffins, giving a wonderful vibrant colour, as well as a sweet, earthy flavour.

Preheat the oven to 190°C/375°F/Gas mark 5. Line a 12-hole muffin tin with parchment cases.

Place all the dry ingredients in a large bowl and stir until well combined. Add the grated beetroot, raisins and walnuts and stir again. Set aside.

Mash the banana with a fork in a separate bowl, until you have a thick, smooth paste. Add the oil, honey, eggs and soya milk and mix thoroughly. Pour into the dry ingredients and stir with a wooden spoon until well combined.

Divide the mixture between the muffin cases and bake in the oven for 20–25 minutes until the tops look golden and crisp. Insert a skewer into the centre of one of the muffins and it should come out clean. Cool on a wire rack and store in an airtight container for up to 5 days.

Eggs with spicy tomatoes and beans

SERVES 2

2 tbsp olive oil
½ onion, diced
1 clove garlic, crushed
1 red pepper, deseeded
   and sliced
400g tin chopped tomatoes
200g tinned haricot beans,
   rinsed and drained
   (or flageolet beans)
½ fresh red chilli,
   deseeded and chopped
1 tbsp tomato purée
½ tsp hot paprika
Pinch cayenne pepper
2 eggs
1 tbsp chopped flat-leaf
   parsley
Salt and freshly ground
   black pepper

Tinned haricot beans are a great store-cupboard staple, but make sure you buy the ones in plain water with no added sugar or salt.

Heat the olive oil in a large frying pan over a medium heat. Add the onion and sauté for a few minutes until it begins to soften. Add the garlic and red pepper and cook for 5 minutes until softened.

Stir in the tomatoes and beans and then add the chopped red chilli, tomato purée, paprika and cayenne pepper. Reduce the heat and simmer for a further 15 minutes, stirring regularly, until the mixture has reduced down by half.

Season with a little salt and plenty of black pepper, then the crack the eggs directly into the tomato mixture. Cook for 10 minutes, or until the egg whites are firm, the yolks still runny and the sauce has reduced slightly. Garnish with the chopped parsley and serve immediately.

Chickpea and spinach frittata

SERVES 2

2 tbsp stanol spread
1 small onion, finely chopped
2 cloves garlic, crushed
2 chargrilled red peppers
　in oil, drained and diced
400g tin chickpeas,
　rinsed and drained
1 tsp smoked paprika
1 tbsp harissa paste
100g bag ready-washed
　baby spinach
4 large eggs, beaten
Salt and freshly ground
　black pepper

Chickpeas and eggs both contain decent protein levels that help to keep you fuller for longer, making this a perfect brunch option. This frittata is delicious hot or cold, so if you have any leftovers you can enjoy a slice for lunch the next day with some salad leaves.

Heat the stanol spread in a small frying pan over a medium heat and sauté the onion and garlic for 10 minutes, until soft. Add the red peppers, chickpeas, paprika and harissa paste. Sauté everything together for about 5 minutes.

Add the spinach and stir through the chickpeas until it wilts and everything is well combined. Add the eggs and seasoning and stir gently, tipping the pan from side to side until the eggs are well incorporated. Allow to set over a medium heat – this should take just 2 minutes.

Preheat the grill to hot, then slide the whole pan under the grill for a couple of minutes until the top is golden in colour.

Kedgeree

• •

SERVES 4

140g brown basmati rice
3 eggs
4 tbsp stanol spread
1 onion, chopped
1 red chilli, deseeded
    and chopped
2 tbsp curry powder
1 tsp black mustard seeds
1 tsp cayenne pepper
100g firm tofu, cubed
2 small smoked mackerel
    fillets, flaked
4 spring onions, sliced
Handful flat-leaf parsley,
    chopped
Salt and freshly ground
    black pepper

Kedgeree is a great weekend breakfast or brunch option and is surprisingly cheap to make. If you are new to tofu this is a good place to start – it's a clever way to get a dose of soya in a familiar dish.

Put the rice in a pan with 280ml of cold water and a pinch of salt. Bring up to the boil, stir, cover and reduce the heat. Simmer gently for 15–20 minutes, or until all the liquid has been absorbed. Alternatively, follow the instructions on the packet.

Meanwhile, boil the eggs in a separate pan for 7 minutes. Drain and set aside.

Heat 2 tablespoons of the stanol spread in a non-stick frying pan over a medium heat. Add the onion and chilli and cook for 5–10 minutes, or until the onion is soft and translucent. Add the curry powder, mustard seeds and cayenne pepper. Fry for a further 1–2 minutes.

Drain the rice well and stir into the spicy onion mix. Add the remaining stanol spread, tofu, mackerel along with the spring onions and most of the parsley. Season well to taste, then heat through gently for a few minutes until piping hot.

Peel and quarter the boiled eggs. Divide the kedgeree between serving bowls and top with the egg quarters and extra parsley.

Oat-crusted kippers with eggs, mushrooms and spinach

SERVES 2

60g porridge oats
3 eggs
2 large kipper fillets, skinned
2 tbsp rapeseed oil
Juice of 1 lemon
100g mushrooms, sliced
150g bag ready-washed
    baby spinach leaves
Pinch ground nutmeg
2 tbsp olive oil
2 tbsp pine nuts, toasted
Salt and freshly ground
    black pepper

Kippers are a firm favourite when it comes to weekend breakfasts and they are high in omega-3 fats and vitamins D and B12. Using porridge oats as a coating for fish gives a similar texture to breadcrumbs but gives you an extra dose of goodness.

Sprinkle the oats on to a plate and season with salt and pepper. Beat one of the eggs in a shallow bowl. Dip each kipper fillet into the egg, then roll it in the seasoned oats. Repeat this process to use up all the oats, making sure the kippers are well coated.

Heat the rapeseed oil in a frying pan over a medium heat and add the coated kipper fillets. Fry for 2–3 minutes on each side, turning carefully, or until crisp and golden-brown on both sides. Remove the pan from the heat and squeeze over the lemon juice.

Meanwhile, place the sliced mushrooms on a baking sheet and place under a hot grill for 6–8 minutes. Put the spinach in a pan with a splash of boiling water and cook over a medium heat until just wilted. Poach the remaining eggs in a separate small pan of boiling water.

When ready to serve, drain the spinach and season with salt and pepper and a pinch of nutmeg. Drizzle over the olive oil and sprinkle over the pine nuts. Tip the grilled mushrooms and the released juices over the spinach and divide between two plates. Top each one with an egg and serve with the kippers.

FUSS-FREE LUNCHES

Mexican hash

SERVES 2

280g baby new potatoes, halved
3 tbsp rapeseed oil
1 clove garlic, chopped
Pinch cayenne pepper
½ tsp ground cinnamon
1 tsp Cajun seasoning
200g tinned sweetcorn, rinsed and drained
200g tinned black beans, rinsed and drained
2 eggs
1 ripe avocado, chopped
½ red chilli, sliced into rounds
1 tbsp chopped fresh coriander (optional)
1 lime, quartered
Salt and freshly ground black pepper

Apart from the avocado, all the ingredients for this spicy dish are store-cupboard staples, making this a great recipe to make for a quick lunch. If you prefer a super spicy kick, simply increase the amount of Cajun seasoning.

Cook the potatoes in a pan of boiling salted water for 5 minutes, or until just tender. Drain well and set aside.

Heat half the rapeseed oil in a pan over a medium heat and fry the potatoes for about 10–15 minutes until golden. Add the garlic, spices, sweetcorn and black beans and heat through for about 5 minutes; season to taste. Keep warm while you fry the eggs.

Heat the remaining oil in a small frying pan and fry the eggs until cooked to your liking. Divide the hash between two bowls and top each one with a fried egg, some chopped avocado, the sliced chilli and chopped coriander, if using. Serve with lime wedges.

Chickpea, hazelnut, sweet potato and butternut salad

. . . .

SERVES 2

250g sweet potato,
    peeled and diced
250g butternut squash,
    peeled and diced
4 tbsp olive oil
200g tinned chickpeas,
    rinsed and drained
60g blanched hazelnuts
2 handfuls watercress leaves
12 cherry tomatoes, halved
2 spring onions, chopped
½ cucumber, chopped
2 tbsp balsamic vinegar

This colourful, fresh and sweet-tasting salad makes a good summer lunch on its own but it will also work well as an accompaniment to a barbecue.

Preheat the oven to 200°C/400°F/Gas mark 6.

Place the sweet potato and butternut squash in a pan, cover with boiling water and simmer for 5–6 minutes until tender. Drain well and then spread out on a baking sheet. Drizzle with half the olive oil and bake in the oven for 15 minutes until browned at the edges. Allow to cool.

Transfer the baked sweet potato and butternut squash to a large bowl and add the chickpeas, hazelnuts, watercress, tomatoes, spring onions and cucumber. Toss together and dress with the remaining olive oil and balsamic vinegar.

Baked sweet potato
with spicy chickpeas

SERVES 2

2 large sweet potatoes, scrubbed

400g tin chickpeas, rinsed and drained

2 tbsp olive oil

1 tsp cayenne pepper

2 large tomatoes, cut into wedges

2 spring onions, sliced

2 tbsp stanol spread

Sweet potatoes provide more fibre as long as you eat the skin too. Swapping the traditional cheese filling for chickpeas makes this a nutrition-packed lunch, although it also works well as a side dish to simple grilled fish.

Preheat the oven to 200°C/400°F/Gas mark 6.

Prick the potatoes in several places and bake for 50 minutes until soft.

Meanwhile, pat the chickpeas dry with kitchen paper. Transfer to a baking sheet, drizzle with half the olive oil and sprinkle with cayenne pepper and bake in the oven for 15 minutes.

In a bowl mix together the tomatoes, spring onions and roasted chickpeas and remaining olive oil. When the sweet potatoes are cooked, cut a cross in the top of each one and add the stanol spread and chickpea filling.

Avocado and bean wrap

SERVES 1

½ ripe avocado
1 wholemeal tortilla wrap
200g tinned refried beans
1–2 jalepeño peppers,
   finely chopped
1 tbsp extra virgin olive oil
Large handful of mixed
   salad leaves

Beans are a versatile source of fibre and you can easily buy refried beans and wraps in most supermarkets. This takes minutes to make and is a really useful recipe to have to hand when you want a quick, healthy lunch.

Scoop out the flesh from the avocado half, place in a bowl and mash with a fork until you have a chunky paste. Spread the avocado over the tortilla.

Spoon the refried beans into a bowl and stir through the chopped peppers and olive oil. Spread evenly over the avocado. Scatter the salad leaves over the top and then roll up the wrap.

Trout and horseradish pâté

· ·

SERVES 1

1 skinless and boneless
  trout fillet
100ml unsweetened
  soya milk
2 tbsp soft soya cheese
Squeeze lemon juice
1 tsp hot horseradish sauce
3–4 oatcakes or 1–2 slices
  seeded wholemeal bread,
  for serving
Pinch salt and freshly
  ground black pepper

Horseradish is my go-to ingredient as it can transform even the most basic dishes. Look for a sugar-free horseradish sauce if you can find it.

Put the trout fillet in a small, shallow pan and pour over the soya milk. Place over a medium heat and bring to a gentle simmer. Cover, reduce the heat to low and poach gently until the fish is cooked through and flakes easily, about 5–8 minutes.

Remove the fillet from the pan with a slotted spoon and place in a bowl. Allow to cool for a few minutes and then add the remaining ingredients. Blend until you have a rough pâté, either by mashing with a fork or by using a hand-held blender. Chill in the fridge until needed; it will keep for 1–2 days. Serve spread on oatcakes or toasted wholemeal bread.

Feta and pomegranate couscous with almonds

SERVES 2

50g frozen edamame
  (green soya beans)
100g couscous
200ml hot chicken
  or vegetable stock
40g flaked almonds
1 pomegranate or 100g
  pomegranate seeds
½ yellow pepper,
  deseeded and diced
½ apple, peeled and grated
10 cherry tomatoes, halved
10 black olives, pitted
  and halved
50g feta-style soya cheese,
  diced
2 tbsp olive oil
Handful flat-leaf parsley,
  chopped
Freshly ground black pepper

If you haven't tried cheese made with soya then give this recipe a go – it's delicious. Soya cheese is available from healthfood stores or online. Couscous is easy to prepare and is a wonderful base for salads as it really soaks up the flavours of other ingredients.

Place the frozen edamame in a pan of water and bring to the boil. Simmer for 1–2 minutes and then drain well.

Put the couscous into a bowl and pour over the hot stock. Cover with cling film and then leave for 5 minutes until the couscous has swelled and absorbed all of the stock. Fluff up with a fork to separate the grains.

Put the flaked almonds in a dry frying pan and toast over a medium-high heat until golden brown. Tip out and allow to cool.

If using whole pomegranate, cut it in half and, holding each half over the bowl of couscous, firmly tap the skin with a rolling pin to extract the seeds. Add all the remaining ingredients, except the parsley, and toss gently together. Season with black pepper to taste. Serve with the chopped parsley scattered over the top.

Nut and bean tabbouleh

SERVES 4

100g bulgar wheat
2 large tomatoes
1 small red onion,
    thinly sliced
Large bunch fresh flat-leaf
    parsley, chopped
Bunch fresh mint, leaves
    roughly chopped
60g walnuts
400g tin haricot beans,
    rinsed and drained
Juice of 1 lemon
4 tbsp olive oil
Salt and freshly ground
    black pepper

Tabbouleh is easy and quick to make and, like couscous, is a great base for other flavours. Fresh mint and parsley give this salad a fresh tangy flavour that works well on its own, although it would also make a great accompaniment to grilled chicken or fish.

Place the bulgar wheat into a bowl and pour over 200ml of boiling water from the kettle. Stir well and cover with cling film. Set aside for 15–20 minutes, or until all the water has been absorbed.

Use a sharp knife to make a small cross at the base of each tomato. Place them in a bowl, cover with boiling water and leave for 30 seconds. Remove carefully with a slotted spoon and set aside. When cool enough to handle, peel away and discard the skins, then chop the tomatoes, removing the seeds first. Transfer to a serving bowl. Add the sliced red onion and herbs to the tomatoes and stir until well combined.

Fluff the cooked bulgar wheat up with a fork until all the grains are separated. Add to the tomato, onion and herb mixture and then stir in the walnuts and haricot beans.

Drizzle over the lemon juice and olive oil and add seasoning to taste. Mix well so that all the ingredients are coated in the dressing.

Smoked mackerel salad

SERVES 4

450g small golden beetroot
3 oranges (use blood oranges
    if you can find them)
2 red or pink apples, cored
    and quartered
1 large head of chicory
4 spring onions, sliced
    diagonally
4 large smoked mackerel
    fillets
120g walnuts

For the dressing
2 tbsp red wine vinegar
2 tbsp freshly squeezed
    orange juice
Zest of ½ orange
5 tbsp olive oil
Pinch salt and freshly
    ground black pepper

This is a really colourful salad; the combination of oranges, apples, beetroot and chicory complement the strong flavour of the smoked fish. Mackerel, with its high levels of omega-3, is particularly beneficial.

Preheat the oven to 200°C/400°F/Gas mark 6. Put the beetroot in a roasting tin with a couple of centimetres of water in the bottom. Cover with foil and roast in the oven for 30 minutes.

Meanwhile, put all the dressing ingredients into a screw-top jar and shake until well combined.

Remove the beetroot from the oven – they should be tender when pierced with a knife. When they are cool enough to handle, peel off the skins, trim them top and bottom and then slice them into rounds. Toss them in a little of the dressing.

Use a sharp knife to trim the top and bottom off each orange. Stand the oranges upright and trim off the rest of the peel and pith, following the contour of the fruit, then cut each orange into thin slices. Cut the apple quarters into thin slices. Trim the head of chicory and separate the leaves, discarding the outer leaves.

Arrange the chicory leaves in a salad bowl and then add the sliced beetroot, orange, apple and spring onion. Flake the fish on top, add the walnuts and drizzle with the remaining dressing.

Chicken soba noodles

2 bundles soba noodles
    (about 200g)
150g cooked chicken breast
    or diced firm tofu
4 tbsp rapeseed oil
½ red chilli, sliced into rounds
1 carrot, cut into matchsticks
50g mangetout, thinly sliced
1 tbsp sesame seeds
60g cashew nuts
1 tbsp soy sauce

This is a lovely fresh salad that is a good way to use leftover cooked chicken. Soba noodles, made from buckwheat, are also wheat-free. Making this with tofu instead of chicken will add a full dose of soya, which will increase the overall cholesterol-lowering properties of this dish.

Cook the noodles in a pan of boiling water, according to the packet instructions. Drain well. Add half the oil to the drained noodles to prevent them from sticking and set aside. Use two forks to shred the chicken.

Heat the oil in a wok and allow it to get hot before adding the chilli, carrot and mangetout. Stir-fry for a couple of minutes and then add the shredded chicken or tofu and drained noodles. Toss together for a few minutes to heat through.

Just before serving, scatter over the sesame seeds, cashew nuts and finish with a splash of soy sauce.

Chicken and asparagus salad

SERVES 2

2 skinless chicken breasts
1 bundle asparagus (about
    200g), tough ends snapped
    off and discarded
1 red pepper, deseeded
    and sliced
2 tbsp olive oil, for drizzling
4 tbsp unsweetened
    soya yoghurt
2 tbsp light mayonnaise
1 tbsp white wine vinegar
1 tbsp chopped dill
½ clove garlic, crushed
120g bag mixed salad leaves
3 tbsp pine nuts, toasted
Salt and freshly ground
    black pepper

This is a lovely summer salad – it's fresh and light but filling at the same time and chicken is a great, low-fat source of protein.

Preheat the oven to 220°C/425°F/Gas mark 7. Use a sharp knife to make two or three shallow cuts in each chicken breast. Arrange the chicken, asparagus and red pepper in a large, shallow roasting tin and drizzle with oil. Season well and then roast in the oven for about 20 minutes, stirring halfway through, until the chicken is cooked through and the vegetables are tender and starting to caramelise.

In a small bowl, whisk together the soya yoghurt, mayonnaise, vinegar, garlic and dill to make a dressing. Season to taste.

Divide the salad leaves between two plates, scatter over the pine nuts and arrange the chicken and vegetables on top. Serve with the dressing.

Chicken, butter bean and walnut salad

SERVES 2

200g skinless chicken breast,
    cut into 2cm pieces
1 sprig rosemary, leaves
    picked and finely chopped
1 sprig lemon thyme, leaves
    picked and finely chopped
1 clove garlic, finely chopped
1 tbsp olive oil
150g green beans, trimmed
200g tin butter beans,
    rinsed and drained
½ red onion, thinly sliced
60g walnuts

For the dressing
3 tbsp olive oil
Juice of ½ lemon
2 tbsp wholegrain mustard
1 tbsp runny honey
½ clove garlic, crushed

Walnuts contain omega-3 fats similar to those found in fish so they are a good cholesterol-lowering food, especially for non-fish eaters.

Place the chicken, rosemary, lemon thyme, garlic and olive oil in a large bowl and toss together until coated in the oil.

Place a large non-stick frying pan over a medium-high heat and tip in the chicken pieces. Cook, stirring, for about 10 minutes until the chicken is browned on all sides and cooked through.

Meanwhile, bring a large pan of water to the boil and add the green beans. Boil for 2 minutes and then add the butter beans and cook for a further 2 minutes until the green beans are just tender and the butter beans are heated through. Drain well.

Make the dressing by whisking together the olive oil, lemon juice, mustard, honey and crushed garlic in a small bowl.

Mix together the warm chicken, beans, sliced red onion and walnuts in a shallow serving bowl. Pour over the dressing and toss gently.

CLEVER
SNACKS

●●●●●●

Hummus three ways

While not all of these recipes can be described as hummus in the traditional sense, this trio of colourful hummus-style dips are packed with flavour and will keep in the fridge for 2–3 days. Here we have chosen to serve these with wholemeal pitta bread, but oatcakes are equally delicious.

1 Beetroot hummus

MAKES 8 SERVINGS

500g raw beetroot, leaves trimmed
2 x 400g tins chickpeas, rinsed and drained
Juice of 2 lemons
1 tbsp ground cumin
4 tbsp olive oil, plus extra for drizzling
1 tbsp Greek yoghurt or unsweetened soya yoghurt
1 tsp cumin seeds or black cumin seeds
1 wholemeal pitta bread per person, to serve
Salt and freshly ground black pepper

Hummus has a reputation for being high in fat but this clever take on the traditional recipe offers fibre, healthy oil, colour and flavour.

Bring a large pan of water to the boil and add the beetroot. Return to the boil, cover, reduce the heat and cook for 50–60 minutes or until soft: a skewer or knife should go all the way through the beetroot easily. Drain and set aside to cool.

Peel the beetroot, discarding the roots (you may want to wear rubber gloves to prevent your hands from staining). Roughly chop the beetroot and then place into a food processor along with the chickpeas, lemon juice, ground cumin and olive oil. Whizz together until you have a coarse paste. Season with a pinch of salt and pepper.

Transfer to a serving bowl and then swirl through the yoghurt. Drizzle over a little more olive oil. Lightly toast the cumin seeds in a dry frying pan for about 30 seconds and then sprinkle over the top of the hummus. Serve with wholemeal pitta bread.

2 Minted pea and soya bean hummus

SERVES 4

100g frozen petits pois
100g frozen edamame
(green soya beans)
100g artichoke hearts
(from a jar), drained
2 tsp ground cumin
2 tbsp lemon juice
4 tbsp olive oil, plus extra
for drizzling
Small handful mint leaves
1 wholemeal pitta bread
per person, to serve
Salt and freshly ground
black pepper

This is a versatile and useful dip that can also be served as a dip with fresh crunchy vegetables or alongside a piece of simple grilled chicken or fish.

Tip the peas and edamame into a bowl and pour over enough boiling water to cover. Leave for 5 minutes, then drain well and tip into a food processor.

Add all the remaining ingredients and pulse to make a rough purée. Season to taste and then spoon into a bowl, drizzle with oil and serve with pitta bread.

3 Macadamia nut hummus

SERVES 4

180g macadamia nuts,
soaked in water for 24
hours, rinsed and drained
2–3 cloves garlic
3 tbsp lemon juice
4 tbsp rapeseed oil, plus
extra for drizzling
2 tbsp tahini
1–2 pinches cayenne pepper
1 wholemeal pitta bread
per person, to serve
Sea salt and freshly
ground pepper

This tangy, fresh-tasting hummus is made with macadamia nuts, which are rich in unsaturated fats. Tahini is a Middle Eastern paste made from ground sesame seeds and so adds a little more unsaturated fat and fibre.

Place all the ingredients into a food processor and blend until you have a smooth paste. Add a little water to loosen if necessary.

Taste and adjust the seasoning and then transfer to a bowl, drizzle with oil, sprinkle with a pinch of cayenne and serve with pitta bread.

Olive bread sticks

MAKES 12

350g strong white bread flour
1 level tsp salt
7g sachet fast-action yeast
180ml lukewarm water
2 tbsp olive oil
300g pitted green olives
Extra virgin olive oil and
  balsamic vinegar, to serve

These are the perfect pre-dinner snack and dipping them into extra virgin olive oil ensures you get the benefit of one of your six foods. They also make a great accompaniment to hummus (see pages 72–73).

Use an electric mixer fitted with a dough hook. Place the flour into the bowl and add the salt, yeast and three-quarters of the water. Mix on a slow speed. As the dough starts to come together, slowly add the rest of the water, while still mixing. Increase the speed and mix for another 5–8 minutes, until the dough is wet and easy to stretch. Add the oil and mix for a further 2 minutes before adding the olives. Stir though with a spoon until evenly distributed.

Place the dough into a large bowl or plastic tub that you have lightly oiled and cover with cling film. Allow to prove for 1 hour.

Towards the end of the proving time, preheat the oven to 220°C/425°F/Gas mark 7. Turn the dough out on to a heavily floured work surface and dust the top of the dough with more flour. Gently stretch the dough into a rectangle about 36 x 25cm and 1cm thick, taking care not to knock too much air out of the dough. Use a sharp knife to cut it into 12 even strips. Place the sticks on to a lightly floured non-stick baking sheet and bake in the oven for 10–15 minutes. Serve with a bowl of olive oil swirled with balsamic vinegar, or for dipping into hummus.

Roasted seeds and soya beans

MAKES 8 SERVINGS

200g frozen edamame
   (green soya beans),
   defrosted
2 tsp olive oil
½ tsp chilli powder
½ tsp dried basil
¼ tsp onion powder
¼ tsp ground cumin
Pinch paprika
Pinch freshly ground
   black pepper
4 tbsp mixed seeds,
   such as pumpkin,
   sunflower, sesame

Crunchy and moreish, these are great to munch on between meals – they also make a very tasty pre-dinner snack with drinks.

Preheat the oven to 190°C/375°F/Gas mark 5. Place the edamame into a mixing bowl, drizzle with the olive oil, then sprinkle with chilli powder, dried basil, onion powder, cumin, paprika and black pepper. Toss until the beans are evenly coated with the oil and spices.

Spread out on to a large baking tray in a single layer. Bake uncovered in the oven for about 12–15 minutes, or until the beans start to turn golden brown, stirring once halfway through cooking. Remove from the oven, allow to cool and then transfer to a bowl. Stir through the mixed seeds.

Cheese, apple and walnut scones

SERVES 12

180g self-raising
  wholemeal flour
Pinch salt
125g stanol spread,
  cut into small pieces
125g grated Cheddar-style
  soya cheese, plus extra
  for sprinkling
180g walnuts, roughly
  chopped
1 apple, peeled, cored
  and diced
3 eggs, beaten

These savoury scones rival traditional jam and cream scones any day. They are a tasty and healthy snack but can also be served alongside soup. Make them in advance and freeze them for up to a month – simply pull out and pop into a preheated oven for 5 minutes to heat through.

Preheat the oven to 180°C/350°F/Gas mark 4 and lightly grease a 12-hole muffin tin. Sift the flour and salt into a mixing bowl, adding the bran pieces left in the sieve to the bowl.

Add the stanol spread and rub into the flour with your fingertips until the mixture looks like coarse crumbs. Gently stir in the cheese, walnuts and apple pieces. Add the beaten eggs to the flour mixture and stir with a wooden spoon to make a stiff mixture.

Spoon the mixture evenly into each hole in the muffin tin. Sprinkle with grated cheese and bake in the oven for 25–30 minutes until golden and cooked through. To check if they are done, insert a skewer into the centre of one of the scones – if it comes out clean it is cooked through. If not, return to the oven for a further 5–10 minutes. Remove from the oven and allow to cool on a wire rack. Serve warm with stanol spread or butter.

Oatcake toppings

* *

Plain oatcakes are the perfect snack standby. Rough oatcakes contain a little more fibre than the smooth variety but still provide plenty of beta-glucan.

1 Oatcakes with spicy satay chicken

SERVES 1

1 tsp ginger paste
1 tsp lemongrass paste
1 tsp honey
1 tsp soy sauce
Squeeze of lime juice
Pinch chilli powder
2 tbsp peanut butter
100g cooked chicken, diced
1 spring onion, thinly sliced
3–4 oatcakes, to serve

You can whip up the topping in advance and keep it covered in the fridge for up to 2 days. Then simply remove it from the fridge about 15 minutes before serving to allow the chicken to soften a little.

Put all the ingredients except the chicken, spring onion and oatcakes into a bowl and whizz together using a hand-held blender. Add the cooked chicken and stir through until they are well coated. Cover with cling film and leave to chill in the fridge.

When ready to serve, pile on to the oatcakes and scatter with the sliced spring onion.

2 Oatcakes with sardine pâté

SERVES 1

120g tin sardines in oil
3 tbsp soya soft cheese
Juice of ½ lemon
Cucumber slices, to serve
3–4 oatcakes, to serve
Freshly ground black pepper

Sardines are a good source of omega-3 oils, which add to the cardiovascular benefits of this simple pâté. You can use fresh sardines when they are available in the summer, but tinned are equally good.

Drain the sardines and place in a bowl. Mash roughly with a fork and then add the soft cheese and lemon juice. Stir well or use a hand-held blender to make a smooth pâté. Season with pepper and chill in the fridge for up to 2 days, until ready to serve.

Pile on to the oatcakes and top each one with slices of cucumber.

3 Oatcakes with mashed bean dip

SERVES 4

400g tin cannellini beans, rinsed and drained
200g feta-style soya cheese
1 tbsp lemon juice
1 clove garlic, crushed
3 tbsp finely chopped fresh dill, mint or chives (or 1 tbsp of each)
3–4 oatcakes, to serve
Freshly ground black pepper

Feta cheese has a grainy texture that's perfect when combined with the smooth texture of cannellini beans.

Tip the beans into a food processor and add the feta, lemon juice and garlic and whizz until smooth. Stir through the chopped herbs and season with black pepper. Chill in the fridge for up to 2 days.

Pile on to the oatcakes and serve.

Red pepper and goat's cheese muffins

SERVES 12

300g wholemeal flour
2 tsp baking powder
1 tsp bicarbonate of soda
Pinch salt
½ tsp cayenne pepper
1 red pepper, deseeded
    and diced
150g soya goat's style
    cheese, diced
1 egg, beaten
270ml unsweetened
    soya milk
100ml rapeseed or
    olive oil

Homemade muffins are easier to make than you might think and this recipe, using wholemeal flour and soya goat's cheese, makes a delicious cholesterol-busting snack.

Preheat the oven to 190°C/375°F/Gas mark 5. Sift the flour, baking powder, bicarbonate of soda, salt and cayenne pepper into a bowl, adding the bran pieces left in the sieve to the bowl.

Add the red pepper and cheese and mix thoroughly using a wooden spoon and then make a well in the centre. Mix together the beaten egg, soya milk and oil in a measuring jug and pour gradually into the flour mixture, stirring with a wooden spoon until combined.

Spoon evenly into a non-stick 12-hole muffin tin or into 12 paper cases arranged on a baking tray. Bake in the oven for 30 minutes until golden brown and a skewer inserted into the centre of a muffin comes out clean. Cool on a wire rack.

WEEKDAY SUPPERS

Broccoli and cashew nut stir-fry

SERVES 4

60g unsalted cashew nuts
1–2 tbsp rapeseed oil
1 head broccoli, cut into
    small florets
4 cloves garlic, sliced
1 red chilli, deseeded and
    thinly sliced
1 bunch spring onions, sliced
200g edamame (green
    soya beans)
2 heads pak choi, quartered
1 tbsp hoisin sauce
1 tbsp soy sauce

For the marinated tofu
1–2 tbsp soy sauce
1 tsp sesame oil
1 clove garlic, crushed
Pinch salt
300g firm tofu,
    cut into cubes

Tofu is a wonderful ingredient: high-protein, cholesterol-free and low in saturated fats. It also has the ability to soak up other flavours beautifully. Roasting cashews yourself is easy and deepens their nutty flavour – you also avoid the excess salt found in ready-toasted cashews.

Preheat the oven to 170°C/325°F/Gas mark 3.

Make the marinated tofu. Put the soy sauce, sesame oil, crushed garlic and salt in a bowl and mix well to combine. Add the tofu cubes and toss until the pieces are coated in the dressing. Set aside to marinate for 10–15 minutes.

Meanwhile, spread the cashews in an even layer on a baking tray and place in the oven. After 5 minutes give them a stir and return to the oven for a further 5–10 minutes – they should be golden brown. Allow to cool.

Remove the tofu cubes from the marinade and drain on kitchen paper. Heat a tablespoon of rapeseed oil in a non-stick wok over a high heat and add the tofu. Cook for a few minutes until golden, then remove from the pan and set aside.

Add the broccoli to the wok, adding a little more oil if necessary, and fry for 5 minutes or until just tender. Add a splash of water if it begins to catch. Add the garlic and chilli and fry for 1 minute before adding the spring onions, edamame, pak choi and fried tofu pieces. Stir-fry for 3–5 minutes and then add the hoisin and soy sauces and toasted cashews. Stir to warm through before serving.

Spicy bean soup

SERVES 4

2 tbsp olive oil
2 onions, sliced
1 clove garlic, crushed
1 red pepper, deseeded
and diced
2 red chillies, sliced
into rounds
2 tsp ras el hanout
1 tsp cumin seeds
400g tin chopped tomatoes
400g tin kidney beans
in chilli sauce
400g tinned butter beans,
rinsed and drained
1 litre hot chicken stock
200g firm tofu
Small bunch fresh coriander,
chopped

I am a big fan of soups, especially if they are a meal in themselves. This spicy and warming soup really hits the spot and is packed with tofu. Ras el hanout is a spice mix used in Moroccan cuisine – it's available from large supermarkets.

Heat half the oil in a large pan over a medium heat. Add the onions, garlic, red pepper, chillies, ras el hanout and cumin seeds to the pan and fry for about 5 minutes until the onions start to soften and turn golden.

Add the tomatoes, kidney beans, butter beans and hot stock and bring to the boil. Reduce the heat and leave to simmer gently, half-covered with a lid, for about 20 minutes.

Pat the tofu dry with kitchen paper. Cut into 2cm size cubes. Heat the remaining oil in a separate pan and add the tofu pieces. Brown on all sides and then remove with a slotted spoon and drain on kitchen paper.

Add the browned tofu pieces to the soup and cook for a further 2 minutes. Spoon into soup bowls and scatter over the chopped coriander before serving.

Goat's cheese, asparagus and soya bean risotto

SERVES 4

4 tbsp stanol spread
1 onion, finely diced
300g risotto rice
1 litre hot vegetable stock
1 bundle (250g) asparagus
   spears, trimmed and sliced
1 glass dry white wine
200g frozen edamame
   (green soya beans)
125g soft goat's cheese
Salt and freshly ground
   black pepper

Goat's cheese might not be the first food you think of when trying to lower your cholesterol but goat's cheese contains around 30 per cent less fat than cow's cheese.

Put the stanol spread in a large, heavy-based pan over a medium heat. Add the onion and cook gently for about 10 minutes or until soft and translucent. Increase the heat a little and stir in the risotto rice, making sure each grain is coated. Cook the rice for 1–2 minutes, or until the grains become translucent at the outer edges.

Add a ladleful of the hot stock to the rice and stir through; reduce the heat slightly. Cook, stirring continuously until all of the liquid has been absorbed. Repeat until the rice is tender and the stock has been used; this should take 18–20 minutes.

Meanwhile, steam the asparagus spears for about 7 minutes until tender. Slice into 2cm lengths.

Once all the stock is absorbed, add the wine, asparagus pieces and edamame. Increase the heat and stir for a few minutes to heat through.

Just before serving, dot the risotto with three-quarters of the goat's cheese, giving it a stir to slightly mix the cheese through. Season and serve immediately with the remaining goat's cheese dotted over the top.

Mushroom and quinoa risotto

SERVES 4

15g dried porcini mushrooms
300ml boiling water
900ml chicken or
   vegetable stock
4 tbsp stanol spread
200g white closed cup
   mushrooms, sliced
200g brown closed cup
   mushrooms, sliced
1 onion, chopped
2 cloves garlic, crushed
175g quinoa
175g risotto rice
100ml dry white wine
200g edamame (green soya
   beans), defrosted if frozen
20g freshly grated Parmesan,
   plus a few extra shavings
2 tbsp chopped fresh
   thyme leaves

Combining quinoa with risotto rice gives this a great texture, a nutty flavour and extra protein too. Serve with a side salad topped with mixed seeds for some added crunch.

Place the dried mushrooms in a bowl, cover with the boiling water and leave to soak for 10 minutes. Drain, reserving the liquid, and chop the mushrooms.

Place the stock in a large saucepan, add the mushroom soaking liquid and slowly bring to the boil; reduce the heat and leave on a gentle simmer.

Heat half the stanol spread in another large saucepan, add the white and brown mushrooms and fry over a high heat for 2–3 minutes until golden brown. Remove from the pan and set aside.

Add the remaining stanol spread to the pan and sauté the onion for 2–3 minutes over a medium heat. Add the chopped dried mushrooms, garlic, quinoa and rice and stir for 30 seconds. Add the wine and gently simmer, stirring until all the liquid has evaporated. Add a ladleful of the hot stock to the rice mixture and cook, stirring until the liquid has been absorbed. Repeat until the rice is tender and the stock has all been used; this should take about 15–20 minutes.

Add the reserved sliced mushrooms, edamame, Parmesan and thyme leaves and stir gently until heated through. Serve immediately with a few extra shavings of Parmesan.

Spinach and chickpea gratin

SERVES 4

4 slices wholemeal bread
450g spinach leaves
2 tbsp rapeseed oil
4 red onions, roughly
   chopped
2 cloves garlic, thinly sliced
2 tbsp plain flour
400g tin chickpeas,
   rinsed and drained
300ml vegetable stock
300g unsweetened
   soya yoghurt
4 large tomatoes, sliced
50g Parmesan, grated
60g chopped hazelnuts
Salt and freshly ground
   black pepper

This is a great vegetarian dish, offering plenty of cholesterol-lowering foods in one pot. It's equally delicious when cold, so keep some for lunch the following day to eat alongside a crisp salad.

Preheat the oven to 180°C/350°F/Gas mark 4. Put the bread slices in a food processor and whizz until you have coarse breadcrumbs.

Wash the spinach thoroughly with cold water and put it in a pan with just the water clinging to its leaves. Cover and steam for 2–3 minutes until the leaves have wilted. Drain and squeeze out the excess water.

Heat the oil in a large pan over a medium heat and add the onions and garlic. Cook gently for about 10 minutes until the onions are soft and translucent, then stir in the flour. Add the chickpeas, stock and soya yoghurt to the pan, season to taste and stir to warm through. Add the spinach and cook for 1 minute before transferring to a large ovenproof dish. Arrange the sliced tomatoes over the top and then scatter over the grated Parmesan, nuts and breadcrumbs. Bake in the oven for 30–40 minutes, until the top is golden and crunchy.

Citrus salmon salad

SERVES 2

200g new potatoes,
  scrubbed and halved
2 skinless and boneless
  salmon fillets, about
  125g each
4 tbsp rapeseed oil, plus
  extra for the salmon
2.5cm piece fresh ginger,
  peeled and grated
½ red chilli, deseeded
  and finely chopped
2 tsp lemongrass paste
2 tbsp clear honey
Juice of 1 small lemon
2 handfuls mixed
  salad leaves
Handful fresh coriander
  leaves, chopped
60g cashew nuts

Salmon is a fantastic source of heart-healthy omega-3 fats. This zingy salad makes a deliciously quick and easy supper in the summer months, when new potatoes are at their best.

Bring a large pan of salted water to the boil and add the new potatoes. Return to the boil, reduce the heat and simmer for 15 minutes, or until just cooked through. Drain and set aside.

Meanwhile, rub the salmon fillets with a little oil and place a non-stick frying pan over a high heat. Cook the salmon fillets for 5 minutes on each side, turning carefully, until golden and cooked through. Set aside and keep warm.

Make a dressing by whisking together the oil, ginger, chilli, lemongrass paste, honey and lemon juice in a small bowl.

Arrange the salad leaves and warm potatoes on two plates and place the salmon fillets on top. Scatter over the chopped coriander and cashew nuts and spoon over the dressing.

Thai tofu and rice noodle soup

SERVES 4

2.5cm piece fresh ginger, peeled and roughly chopped

1–2 red chillies, deseeded and roughly chopped (leave the seeds in for an extra kick)

1–2 stalks lemongrass, outer layers removed, roughly chopped

2–3 cloves garlic

Handful fresh coriander

1–2 tbsp rapeseed oil

1 tbsp coriander seeds

¼ tsp ground turmeric

300ml vegetable stock

100g rice noodles

400ml tin light coconut milk

200g tofu, drained and cut into 2.5cm cubes

200g tinned chickpeas, rinsed and drained

1 tbsp Thai fish sauce, or to taste

The addition of chickpeas here is an excellent way to increase your intake of cholesterol-lowering fibre and makes this otherwise light and superbly fragrant soup a bit more substantial.

Put the ginger, chillies, lemongrass, garlic and coriander in a food processor, reserving a few sprigs of coriander for the garnish. Whizz until you have a chunky paste, adding a little rapeseed oil if the paste is too dry.

Tip the paste into a large pan and cook over a medium heat for a few minutes to release the aromas, stirring frequently. Roughly crush the coriander seeds with a pestle and mortar and add to the paste with the turmeric and vegetable stock. Bring to a simmer and cook for 2–3 minutes.

Meanwhile, put the rice noodles into a bowl and cover them with boiling water. Let them sit until they have softened, about 4–5 minutes, then drain and set aside.

Add the coconut milk to the pan and return to the boil. Reduce the heat and simmer for a few minutes. Add the tofu and chickpeas to the pan and cook for a further 2–3 minutes. Stir in the drained noodles. Chop the reserved fresh coriander sprigs and add to the pan with the fish sauce, to taste.

Serve between warmed serving bowls.

Tuna steak with mango salsa and spicy bean cakes

....

SERVES 2

2 tuna steaks, about
 140–160g each
Olive oil, for drizzling
2 limes, cut into wedges
Salt and freshly ground
 black pepper

For the bean cakes
2 slices wholemeal bread
400g tin kidney beans,
 rinsed and drained
200g tinned butter beans,
 rinsed and drained
200g tinned black-eye
 beans, rinsed and drained
3 tbsp olive oil
1 small onion, finely diced
Handful flat-leaf parsley,
 chopped
1 small red chilli, deseeded
 and finely chopped

For the mango salsa
1 mango, peeled, stoned
 and diced
1 small red onion,
 diced
1 red chilli, deseeded
 and finely chopped
Handful fresh coriander
 leaves, chopped
Handful fresh mint
 leaves, chopped

A perfect dish for summer when mangos are at their best. The bean cakes and salsa can be made several hours in advance.

Make the bean cakes. Whizz the bread in a food processor until you have coarse breadcrumbs. Tip into a large bowl. Add the drained beans to the food processor and pulse to get a rough paste.

Heat 1 tablespoon of the oil in a frying pan over a medium heat and gently fry the onion until softened, about 8–10 minutes. Add the onion to the breadcrumbs along with the blended beans, parsley, chilli, and salt and pepper. Mix until well combined and then divide the mixture into six balls. Use your hands to flatten them into patties. Chill in the fridge.

To make the mango salsa, put all the ingredients into a bowl and mix lightly to combine. Squeeze in the juice of one of the limes. Chill in the fridge until ready to serve.

Heat the remaining olive oil in a large non-stick frying pan. Fry the cakes for 2–3 minutes on each side, or until golden-brown and cooked through. Remove from the pan and drain on kitchen paper.

Meanwhile, drizzle each tuna steak with a little olive oil and rub all over the fish; season well with salt and pepper. Place a ridged griddle pan over a high heat and add the tuna steaks. Cook for 2 minutes, then turn over and cook for 2 minutes on the other side until charred but still a little pink in the middle.

Serve the tuna steaks with the spicy bean cakes, remaining lime wedges and the salsa on the side.

Lemon prawns

SERVES 2

2.5cm piece fresh ginger,
    peeled and grated
½ red chilli, deseeded
    and chopped
1 clove garlic, sliced
Juice of 1 lemon
60g stanol spread
2 leeks, trimmed and sliced
200g cooked tiger prawns
200g tinned cannellini
    beans, rinsed and drained
Small handful chopped
    coriander (optional)
Salt and freshly ground
    black pepper

Fibre-rich beans served alongside seafood is an ideal way to enjoy prawns and shellfish, yet still manage cholesterol levels. You could serve these fragrant, lemony prawns with brown rice to increase your fibre count.

Using a small grinder, processor or pestle and mortar, make a paste with the ginger, chilli, garlic and lemon juice.

Heat the stanol spread in a pan over a medium heat, add the leeks and cook for 3–5 minutes until soft. Tip in the ginger-chilli paste and sauté for a couple of minutes.

Add the prawns and beans and cook for 2 minutes until heated through. Season with salt and pepper to taste and then scatter with the chopped coriander before serving, if using.

Salmon and broccoli penne

SERVES 4

250g wholewheat
   penne pasta
300g broccoli, cut into
   large florets
30g stanol spread
25g plain flour
700ml stanol milk
100g soft soya cheese
8 sun-dried tomatoes in oil,
   drained and thickly sliced
8 anchovy fillets, halved
   (optional)
Handful of fresh basil leaves
250g smoked salmon,
   cut into strips
Freshly ground black pepper

The basis of this pasta dish is a simple white sauce made with milk and soft soya cheese, making it deliciously creamy. The smoked salmon has a naturally salty flavour so don't be tempted to add salt to this dish. Serve with a fresh green salad.

Bring a large pan of salted water to the boil and cook the pasta according to the packet instructions. Add the broccoli florets 4 minutes before the end of the cooking time and continue to cook until the broccoli and pasta are just cooked. Drain well.

While the pasta is cooking, melt the stanol spread in a pan, add the flour and cook for 30 seconds. Gradually stir in the stanol milk and heat gently, whisking or stirring all the time, until it thickens to make a smooth sauce. Remove from the heat and stir in the soft soya cheese, sun-dried tomatoes, anchovies (if using) and basil leaves.

Add the smoked salmon and drained penne and broccoli and stir gently over a medium heat until heated through. Season with pepper and serve immediately.

Fish chowder

SERVES 4

2 tbsp olive oil
2 leeks, thinly sliced
400g celeriac, peeled and
  cut into small cubes
1 parsnip, peeled and diced
1 litre fish stock
Zest of 1 lemon
300ml unsweetened
  soya milk
330g tin sweetcorn,
  rinsed and drained
250g skinless and boneless
  salmon, cut into chunks
250g skinless and boneless
  white fish, such as haddock
  or cod, cut into chunks
Handful chives, snipped
1–2 slices seeded wholemeal
  bread per person, to serve
Salt and freshly ground
  black pepper

This simple chowder is both warming and filling as it's packed with omega-3 fatty acids. Use any firm white fish you have available.

Heat the oil in a large pan over a medium heat, tip in the leeks and fry gently for 5 minutes until softened, but not coloured. Add the celeriac and parsnip and cook for a further minute. Add the stock and lemon zest, cover and simmer for 12–15 minutes or until the vegetables are tender. Using a slotted spoon, remove half the vegetables from the stock and set aside.

Transfer the remaining vegetables and stock to a blender or food processor and whizz until smooth; stir in the soya milk. Return to the pan and add the sweetcorn, fish and reserved vegetables. Cover and gently heat for 3–4 minutes until the fish is just cooked through – take care not to boil. Stir in the chives and add seasoning to taste. Serve with sliced seeded wholemeal bread.

Fruity South African chicken

SERVES 2

2 tbsp olive oil
2 skinless chicken breasts
100g wholegrain basmati rice
1 onion, finely chopped
1 stick celery, thinly sliced
½ red pepper, deseeded
  and thinly sliced
1 tsp hot curry paste
2 tbsp tomato purée
200g tinned apricot halves
  (in juice), drained and
  thickly sliced
60g cashew nuts
100ml white wine or
  chicken stock
Few fresh coriander sprigs,
  to garnish

Cashew nuts and apricots give this chicken dish a wonderful sweet flavour that is nicely balanced by the spices in the curry paste.

Heat the oil in a frying pan over a medium heat and add the chicken breasts. Cook for about 10 minutes on each side, making sure they are thoroughly cooked and starting to brown. Remove from the pan and set aside.

Meanwhile, put the rice into a pan with 200ml of cold water and a pinch of salt. Bring up to the boil, stir, cover and reduce the heat. Simmer gently for 15–20 minutes, or until all the liquid has been absorbed. Alternatively, follow the instructions on the packet.

Add the onion, celery and red pepper to the pan in which you cooked the chicken and cook for 10 minutes until softened. Stir in the curry paste, tomato purée, apricots, cashew nuts and wine or stock and bring to the boil. Reduce the heat and simmer for 5 minutes until the sauce has reduced and thickened. Return the chicken breasts to the pan to heat through and then serve with the rice. Scatter over the fresh coriander to garnish.

Pistachio chicken drumsticks

SERVES 2

Juice of 1 lemon
4 chicken drumsticks,
   skin removed
2 tbsp wholemeal flour
2 tsp curry powder
60g shelled pistachios
Handful fresh coriander
   leaves, roughly torn
Pinch cayenne pepper
2 tbsp rapeseed or olive oil
1 egg, beaten
Salt and freshly ground
   black pepper

Shelled pistachios have a rich green colour and make this an alluring dish to serve as a main course. The drumsticks are crispy and moreish even though the skin has been removed and can be enjoyed with a salad or steamed vegetables.

Preheat the oven to 220°C/425°F/Gas mark 7.

Squeeze the lemon juice over the chicken drumsticks. Mix the flour, curry powder and some seasoning together in a shallow dish. Toss the drumsticks in the flour mixture until well coated on all sides. Tap off the surplus flour and arrange them on a plate, reserving the unused flour.

Put the pistachios, coriander leaves, reserved flour and cayenne pepper in a food processor and pulse until well combined. Tip out on to a shallow plate.

Pour the oil into a roasting tin and swirl to coat the bottom of the tin. Put the tin in the oven to warm while you coat the chicken.

Dip each drumstick into the beaten egg and then into the pistachio mixture ensuring they are well coated. Add the drumsticks to the hot roasting tin, turning to coat in the oil, and cook in the oven for 25–30 minutes, or until cooked through. Drain on kitchen paper and serve with a mixed leaf and tomato salad.

Curried chicken salad

SERVES 2

2 skinless chicken breasts
400g tin chickpeas,
    rinsed and drained
200ml unsweetened
    soya yoghurt
2 tsp mild curry powder
Juice of ½ lemon
Handful mint leaves,
    chopped (reserve a
    few leaves to garnish)
100g cherry tomatoes,
    halved
1 small red onion,
    thinly sliced
60g walnuts
Salt and freshly ground
    black pepper

This salad packs quite a punch in terms of lowering cholesterol and is a good choice for a healthy supper at the end of a busy day. It's also quite rich in protein making it more filling than you might think.

Bring a pan of water to the boil. Season the chicken breasts with a pinch of salt and pepper, then lower into the pan. Put a lid on and reduce the heat to low. Simmer for 15 minutes until the chicken is cooked through.

Remove from the pan with a slotted spoon and, when cool enough to handle, shred the chicken. Place the chicken in a bowl with the chickpeas.

In a small bowl, mix together the soya yoghurt, curry powder, lemon juice and chopped mint. Pour the dressing over the chicken and chickpeas and toss gently to combine; season to taste. Arrange on two plates and scatter over the tomatoes, onion, reserved mint leaves and walnuts.

Harissa chicken

SERVES 2

2 skinless chicken breasts
4 tsp harissa paste
2 tbsp olive oil
60g pine nuts
100g giant couscous
2 spring onions, chopped
¼ cucumber, chopped
2 tomatoes, chopped
200g chickpeas, rinsed
    and drained
30g raisins
Handful flat-leaf parsley,
    chopped
Handful mint, chopped
Extra virgin olive oil,
    to serve

Harissa is a hot, aromatic paste made from chilli and gives this dish a real kick. Giant couscous, with its pearl-like grains, is a great alternative to regular couscous and will give you a decent dose of fibre too.

Preheat the oven to 170°C/325°F/Gas mark 3. Smear each chicken breast with 2 teaspoons of the harissa paste and place in an ovenproof dish. Drizzle over the oil, season with salt and pepper and bake in the oven for 20–25 minutes until cooked through.

Put the pine nuts in a dry frying pan and place over a medium heat for a few minutes to toast – remove from the heat as soon as they turn golden as they can burn quickly.

Bring a pan of salted water to the boil and cook the giant couscous according to the packet instructions (times can vary). Drain and then combine with all the remaining ingredients. Serve each chicken breast on a bed of the couscous salad drizzled with extra virgin olive oil.

Chicken lentil masala

SERVES 2

2 skinless chicken breasts
2 tbsp rapeseed oil
1 red onion, finely chopped
2 tbsp medium curry paste
400g tin chopped tomatoes
1 litre vegetable stock
200g Puy lentils
200g spinach leaves
4 tbsp unsweetened
   soya yoghurt
½ cucumber, chopped
1 tsp cumin seeds
Handful fresh mint leaves,
   chopped, plus extra
   to garnish
Salt and freshly ground
   black pepper

For the marinade
Juice of 1 lemon
1 clove garlic, crushed
1 tsp grated ginger
1 tsp ground cumin
1 tsp crushed cardamom
   pods
Pinch ground cloves
½ tsp fenugreek seeds
½ tsp ground turmeric
½ tsp cayenne pepper

The list of ingredients might appear long, but don't be intimidated as it's actually very easy to make.

Mix together the ingredients for the marinade in a bowl. Place the chicken breasts in a shallow dish, season with the marinade and salt and pepper. Use your hands to rub the mixture into the chicken. Cover with cling film and chill for 3–4 hours, or overnight if possible.

Heat the rapeseed oil in a large frying pan over a medium heat, add the chopped onion and cook for 3–4 minutes until softened. Add the curry paste and cook for 1 minute to release the flavours, then add the tomatoes and vegetable stock and bring to the boil. Add the lentils, reduce the heat and simmer for 40–50 minutes. Remove from the heat and add the spinach leaves, allowing them to wilt in the heat of the pan.

Remove the chicken breasts from the marinade and grill for 7 minutes on each side. Meanwhile mix together the soya yoghurt, cucumber, cumin seeds and chopped mint in a small bowl.

Serve each chicken breast on a bed of lentils and garnish with a few mint leaves. Serve the cucumber yoghurt on the side.

Turkey burgers

SERVES 2

100g turkey breast mince
100g tinned haricot beans,
   rinsed and drained
2 spring onions, chopped
1–2 tsp Thai red curry paste
2 tbsp rapeseed oil
1 tbsp low-fat mayonnaise
2 tbsp unsweetened soya
   yoghurt
1 tbsp chopped fresh
   coriander leaves
2 wholemeal baps
2 tsp English mustard
   (optional)
Handful mixed salad leaves

Turkey is naturally low in fat and is a good alternative to beef when it comes to homemade burgers. Most burger recipes use breadcrumbs but here haricot beans do the trick beautifully, as well as giving you that all-important dose of fibre.

Put the turkey mince, haricot beans, spring onions and curry paste in a bowl and mix together until well combined and the beans are lightly crushed. You may find it easier to use your hands. Divide the mixture into two and then shape into two patties. These can be chilled in the fridge until needed.

Heat the oil in a large frying pan and fry the burgers for 10 minutes, turning occasionally, until golden and cooked through.

Mix together the mayonnaise, soya yoghurt and coriander and spread over one half of each bap. Spread the other half with mustard, if using. Place the burgers in the baps with a few salad leaves and serve immediately.

Pork and apple meatballs

SERVES 4

100g dried soya mince
2 slices seeded wholemeal
  bread
1 large shallot, roughly
  chopped
1 apple, peeled, cored
  and roughly chopped
1 tbsp chopped fresh
  lemon thyme leaves
300g lean pork mince
4 tbsp olive oil
4 tbsp apple sauce
4 tbsp unsweetened
  soya yoghurt
Salt and freshly ground
  black pepper

Pork contains less fat than you might think. In fact, lean pork mince has around 8 per cent fat, compared to the 6 per cent found in chicken, so it's perfectly acceptable to include in your diet from time to time.

Put the soya mince into a bowl and pour over 300ml of boiling water. Leave to soak for about 30 minutes until the water has been absorbed.

Place the bread slices, shallot, apple and lemon thyme in a food processor and whizz until finely chopped. Add to the soya mince along with the pork mince and season with salt and pepper. Mix well to combine and then shape the mixture into small balls, using damp hands so that the mixture doesn't stick.

Heat the olive oil in a large non-stick frying pan and fry the meatballs over a medium heat for 12–15 minutes or until cooked through, turning occasionally to colour evenly. Remove from the pan and drain on kitchen paper.

Mix together the apple sauce and soya yoghurt and serve alongside the hot meatballs.

FAMILY
MEALS

● ● ● ● ● ●

Tomato and spinach macaroni cheese

SERVES 6

175g Cheddar-style soya cheese, grated
70g Parmesan, grated
50g fresh wholemeal breadcrumbs
50g Gruyère, grated
280g macaroni
75g stanol or soya spread, plus extra for greasing
200g spinach leaves, tough stalks removed
50g plain flour
700ml stanol milk
1 tsp Dijon mustard
3 tomatoes, thickly sliced
Freshly ground black pepper

A mac 'n' cheese that has all the flavour of a well-known classic but with cholesterol-lowering properties is very hard to beat. We're sure the family will agree.

Preheat the oven to 190°C/375°F/Gas mark 5 and lightly grease an ovenproof dish, about 30 x 20cm.

Combine 25g of the Cheddar-style cheese and one-third of the Parmesan with the breadcrumbs. In a separate bowl, mix together the rest of the cheeses and set aside.

Cook the macaroni in a pan of salted boiling water according the packet instructions and drain well.

Put one-third of the spread and spinach into a large, lidded saucepan over a medium heat. Cover and cook for about 2 minutes. Drain the spinach in a colander and, once cool enough to handle, squeeze out the excess liquid and then chop roughly.

Heat the stanol milk in a small saucepan. Melt the remaining spread in a saucepan and stir in the flour. Cook for about 30 seconds, stirring, then take off the heat. Gradually pour in the milk, stirring continuously, until you have a smooth sauce.

Put the pan of sauce back on the heat and cook, stirring, until thickened and smooth. Simmer for about 4 minutes until glossy, stirring every now and then. Remove from the heat and stir in the cheeses and mustard. Season to taste with pepper. Stir the macaroni and spinach into the sauce.

Tip the macaroni cheese into the prepared dish and sprinkle over the breadcrumb mixture. Arrange the sliced tomatoes over the top and cook in the oven for 15–20 minutes until golden and bubbling.

Tomato and pesto filo pizza

SERVES 4

2 red onions, cut into wedges
1 red pepper, deseeded
 and roughly chopped
8 cherry tomatoes, halved
Olive oil, for drizzling and
 brushing
4 filo pastry sheets,
 about 30 x 20cm
2–3 tbsp sun-dried
 tomato paste
100g grated soya mozzarella

For the pesto
50g pine nuts
Large handful fresh
 basil leaves
50g Parmesan, grated
150ml olive oil
2 cloves garlic
Salt and freshly ground
 black pepper

This lighter version of pizza is made with filo pastry and can still help manage cholesterol and be full of flavour – the olive oil and pine nuts in the pesto combine two of your cholesterol-lowering foods.

Preheat the oven to 220°C/425°F/Gas mark 7. Put the onions, red peppers and tomatoes into a roasting tin, lightly drizzle with olive oil and roast for 15 minutes or until just tender. Allow to cool slightly.

Lightly oil a baking sheet. Layer the pastry sheets on top of one another on the baking sheet, brushing each one generously with olive oil as you layer. Spread the tomato paste over the top, leaving a 2cm border all around.

Top with the roasted vegetables and grated soya mozzarella and then bake in the oven for 12–15 minutes, until crisp and golden brown.

Meanwhile, place a small frying pan over a low heat. Add the pine nuts and toast until golden, shaking occasionally. Tip them into a food processor with the remaining ingredients for the pesto and process until smooth. Season with salt and pepper.

Just before serving, drizzle 4 tablespoons of the pesto over the pizza. Keep any leftover pesto in the fridge for up to 2 days.

Spinach, ricotta and cashew nut lasagne

SERVES 4

60g stanol spread, plus 1 tbsp
50g plain flour
850ml unsweetened
    soya milk
1 bay leaf
60g Parmesan, grated
120g cashew nuts
600g spinach, tough
    stalks removed
225g ricotta
½ tsp ground nutmeg
100g crumbly blue cheese,
    such as Danish blue
100g grated mozzarella
    or soya mozzarella
12 oven-ready lasagne sheets
Salt and freshly ground
    black pepper

This clever take on a traditional favourite uses soya milk for the sauce and cashew nuts in between layers.

Preheat the oven to 180°C/350°F/Gas mark 4. Melt the stanol spread in a saucepan, add the flour and cook for 30 seconds. Stir in the milk, add the bay leaf and heat gently, stirring continuously, until it thickens. Turn the heat down and simmer gently for 5 minutes. Stir in all but a tablespoon of the Parmesan, then remove the pan from the heat; discard the bay leaf.

Put the cashew nuts on a baking tray and roast in the oven for 5–10 minutes until golden brown. Wash the spinach thoroughly in cold water and shake dry. Put the spread and spinach in a large, lidded saucepan, cover and place over a medium heat for about 2 minutes. Drain the spinach and when it's cool enough to handle, squeeze the excess liquid, then chop roughly. Put it in a bowl, add the ricotta and 150ml of the white sauce. Mix in the nutmeg, some seasoning and the blue cheese.

Assemble the lasagne by spreading a quarter of the sauce into the bottom of a lasagne dish (about 20 x 28cm), then one-third of the spinach mixture, followed by a scattering of toasted cashew nuts, followed by a layer of lasagne sheets. Repeat the whole process, this time adding a third of the grated mozzarella along with the cashew nuts. Repeat again, finishing with a layer of pasta, the rest of the sauce and the remaining Parmesan and mozzarella. Bake for 40 minutes, until the top is golden and bubbling. Serve alongside a green salad.

Fish crumble

75g stanol spread
1 onion, chopped
2 bay leaves
50g plain flour
150ml white wine
250ml unsweetened
    soya milk
500g skinless and boneless
    salmon fillet, cut into
    3cm cubes
400g skinless and boneless
    smoked haddock,
    cut into 3cm cubes
200g peeled prawns
2 tbsp chopped fresh dill
Salt and freshly ground
    black pepper

For the crumble topping
100g stanol spread
150g wholemeal flour
150g oatmeal
50g Parmesan, finely grated
Small bunch flat-leaf parsley,
    finely chopped
1–2 tsp olive oil (optional)

An interesting alternative to fish pie, this crumble offers plenty of omega-3 unsaturated fats. Serve with plenty of crunchy steamed vegetables for extra fibre.

Preheat the oven to 200°C/400°F/Gas mark 6. Melt the stanol spread in a large saucepan over a medium heat and gently sauté the onion with the bay leaves until the onion is softened but not coloured. Stir in the flour and cook for about 30 seconds before gradually adding the wine, stirring to prevent any floury lumps. Add the milk in the same way, bring to a simmer and cook for a few minutes until you have a thick sauce. Remove and discard the bay leaf.

Stir in the salmon, haddock and prawns and return to a simmer, stirring occasionally. Cook for a few minutes, taking care not to break up the fish too much, then add the dill and season with salt and pepper. Spoon into a large ovenproof dish and set aside.

To make the crumble topping melt the stanol spread in a large saucepan, then remove from the heat and stir in the flour, oatmeal, Parmesan and chopped parsley. Add a little olive oil if the mixture seems too dry.

Scatter the topping over the top of the fish and cook in the preheated oven for 30–40 minutes, until the topping is golden and the filling is bubbling at the edges.

Sardine pasta bake

SERVES 4

4 slices wholemeal bread
1 tbsp chopped flat-leaf
   parsley
1 tbsp chopped fresh oregano
Grated zest of 1 lemon
1 tbsp grated Parmesan
1 tbsp olive oil, plus extra
   for drizzling
1 onion, finely chopped
1 large carrot, finely diced
1 stick celery, finely diced
1 green pepper, deseeded
   and cut into strips
250g chestnut mushrooms,
   quartered
4 x 120g tins sardines
   in oil, drained
400g tin chopped tomatoes
1 tbsp tomato purée
1 tsp Italian herb seasoning
300g wholewheat fusilli
   pasta

Sardines are an oily fish that are rich in omega-3 heart-healthy fats but are often overlooked. Here the tomato, mushrooms and herbs combine well with the robust flavour of sardines.

Preheat the oven to 190°C/375°F/Gas mark 5. Put the bread slices in a food processor and whizz until you have coarse breadcrumbs. Add the parsley, oregano, lemon zest and Parmesan and whizz again until everything is well combined and finely chopped.

Heat the oil in a large frying pan and fry the onion over a medium heat until soft, about 5 minutes. Add the carrot, celery, green pepper and mushrooms and cook for 10 minutes. Stir in the sardines, chopped tomatoes, tomato purée and Italian herb seasoning. Continue cooking for 5 minutes, gently breaking up the sardines, until everything is heated through.

Meanwhile, bring a large saucepan of salted water to the boil and cook the pasta according to the packet instructions. Drain and place in an ovenproof dish with a drizzle of olive oil to keep it from sticking. Stir in the sauce and top with the breadcrumb mixture. Bake in the preheated oven for 15 minutes until the top is golden.

Crab and bean fishcakes

SERVES 4

2.5cm piece fresh ginger, peeled and roughly chopped
2 red chillies, deseeded
400g tin butter beans, rinsed and drained
250g white crabmeat
1 tsp Dijon mustard
2 tbsp chopped fresh coriander
2 tbsp chopped fresh mint
2 spring onions, thinly sliced
2 medium eggs
100g wholemeal breadcrumbs
Semolina flour, for dusting
4 tbsp olive or rapeseed oil

The combination of crab with butter beans results in a wonderful texture, as well as that all-important dose of fibre.

Put the ginger and chillies in a small food processor and whizz until finely chopped. Transfer to a bowl and add the butter beans. Use a fork to roughly smash the beans and then add the crabmeat, mustard, chopped coriander and mint and spring onions.

Beat one of the eggs and add to the bowl, and then stir in 40g of the breadcrumbs. Mix until well combined and then divide the mixture into 8 equal portions and shape into patties. Chill in the fridge for about 20 minutes.

When ready to cook, preheat the oven to 180°C/350°F/Gas mark 4. Beat the remaining egg in a bowl. Place some semolina flour and the remaining breadcrumbs in two separate shallow dishes. Dust each fishcake with flour, then dip in the beaten egg and finally the breadcrumbs, making sure they are evenly coated. Shake gently to remove any excess breadcrumbs.

Heat the oil in a frying pan and fry the fishcakes for 2–3 minutes on each side, or until crisp and golden all over. Transfer to a baking tray and cook in the oven for 5–10 minutes, or until hot all the way through. Serve with a fresh green salad.

Pulled pork with refried beans

SERVES 8

For the pulled pork
Olive oil, for greasing
2kg boneless pork shoulder
1 tbsp dried chilli flakes
1 tbsp wholegrain mustard
200ml white wine vinegar
250ml cider
2 onions, thinly sliced
6 cloves garlic, sliced
400g steamed green beans,
    to serve
Salt and freshly ground
    black pepper

For the refried beans
4 tbsp rapeseed oil
2 onions, finely chopped
4 cloves garlic, finely chopped
1 tbsp cumin seeds
4 x 400g tins pinto or kidney
    beans, rinsed and drained
2 tbsp smoked paprika
Salt and freshly ground
    black pepper

This dish involves long, slow cooking so is great for a relaxed Sunday lunch with family and friends. After several hours in the oven you will be met with meltingly tender meat. Served with fibre-rich beans, this indulgent treat is perfectly allowable – just not for every day.

Preheat the oven to 170°C/325°F/Gas mark 3. Place the pork shoulder in a lightly oiled roasting tin into which it fits snugly. Mix together the chilli, mustard and some salt and pepper and then rub all over into the pork shoulder – use your hands to really work the mixture into the skin. Pour over the vinegar and cider and then scatter over the sliced onion and garlic.

Cover with parchment paper and then cover the tin tightly with foil. Cook in the preheated oven for 3 hours. Remove the parchment paper and foil and return to the oven to cook for a further 1 hour.

To 'pull' the pork, first remove the rind and discard. Then use two forks to shred the meat into pieces – it should be soft and tender and fall off the bone.

For the refried beans, heat the oil in a large frying pan and cook the onions and garlic over a medium heat for 2 minutes. Add the cumin seeds and cook for a further minute. Tip in the beans, paprika and a splash of water. Using a potato masher, break the beans down as they warm through to make a rough purée. Season well with salt and pepper. Serve the pork with the refried beans and the steamed green beans.

Turkey pilaf

SERVES 2

60g whole blanched
   hazelnuts
2 tbsp olive oil
1 onion, finely chopped
1 clove garlic, crushed
4 cardamom pods,
   lightly crushed
1 tsp ground cumin
1 tsp ground coriander
1 cinnamon stick
100g brown basmati rice
600–800ml hot vegetable
   stock
200g cooked turkey, shredded
100g edamame (green soya
   beans)
Handful fresh coriander
   leaves, roughly chopped
Salt and freshly ground
   black pepper

A really nice main course that offers plenty of cholesterol-busting ingredients is a clever way to use leftover turkey after a celebration meal, such as Christmas or Easter. This also works well with leftover cooked chicken or marinated tofu for that extra dose of soya.

Place a small frying pan over a medium heat and add the whole hazelnuts. Toast for a few minutes, stirring occasionally, until the nuts turn golden brown. Remove from the pan quickly as they will continue to cook in the pan and can burn easily.

Heat the oil in a large, lidded saucepan and gently fry the onions and garlic over a medium heat until softened, about 5 minutes. Add the cardamom, ground spices and cinnamon stick and stir through the onions for a couple of minutes before adding the rice. Stir-fry for 1–2 minutes, making sure the rice is well combined with the onions and spices.

Cut a circle of greaseproof paper larger than the saucepan lid. Pour in the hot stock and then place the greaseproof paper over the top, followed by the lid. Reduce the heat to low and steam until the stock is nearly all absorbed, about 25–30 minutes. Remove the lid and paper and stir in the turkey, edamame and hazelnuts. Continue to cook until everything is warmed through. Season to taste and then scatter over the coriander just before serving.

Chicken and cashew korma

SERVES 4

4 tbsp rapeseed oil
2 large onions, chopped
2cm piece fresh ginger,
  peeled and chopped
½ tsp cumin seeds
2 tbsp ground coriander
1 tbsp ground cumin
½ tsp turmeric
½ tsp cayenne pepper
5 cloves garlic, crushed
4 skinless chicken breasts,
  diced or 400g firm tofu,
  diced
120g cashew nuts
300ml chicken stock
120g ground almonds
4 tbsp unsweetened soya
  cream or yoghurt
Handful fresh coriander
  leaves
Salt and freshly ground
  black pepper
Cooked brown basmati
  rice, to serve

For many of us Indian food is a much-loved indulgent treat, so this tasty version, packed with cholesterol-lowering nuts, is a revelation. Using tofu instead of chicken will give you an extra dose of soya.

Put the oil in a large saucepan and place over a medium heat. Add the chopped onions and ginger and fry for 3–4 minutes, or until softened. Add the cumin seeds, ground coriander, ground cumin, turmeric and cayenne pepper and fry for 1–2 minutes, until the spices release their aromas. Stir in the crushed garlic and cook for 1 minute more.

Add the chicken or tofu pieces and cashew nuts to the pan. Continue to cook over a medium heat, until the chicken or tofu is lightly browned on all sides. Add some salt and pepper and then pour in the chicken stock. Bring to the boil, then reduce the heat to a simmer and cook gently for about 15 minutes.

Stir the ground almonds into the soya cream or yoghurt and then add to the pan. Stir gently and continue cooking for a further 5 minutes to allow the mixture to heat through. Stir through half the chopped coriander and scatter the rest on top. Serve with brown basmati rice.

Poached chicken and spring vegetables

SERVES 4

4 skinless and boneless chicken thighs, halved
Handful flat-leaf parsley, roughly chopped
4 bay leaves
6 black peppercorns
150g new potatoes, scrubbed
150g baby carrots
150g baby turnips or radishes
1 fennel bulb, quartered, herby tops removed and reserved
2 tbsp creamed horseradish
300ml unsweetened soya yoghurt
50g frozen peas
200g frozen edamame (green soya beans)
100g Swiss chard, chopped
Salt and freshly ground black pepper

This wonderfully light dish is packed full of healthy spring vegetables, including those all-important edamame (green soya beans). Served with a peppery horseradish yoghurt sauce, it's sublime.

Season the chicken with black pepper and place into a large pan. Cover with water and add a good pinch of salt. Add the parsley, bay leaves, peppercorns and potatoes, place over a high heat and bring to the boil. Reduce the heat, cover and simmer for about 20 minutes. Add the baby carrots, turnips or radishes and fennel and simmer for a further 30–40 minutes.

Combine the creamed horseradish and soya yoghurt in a bowl and set aside.

Remove the chicken from the pan with a slotted spoon and transfer to a bowl. Remove and discard the whole peppercorns. Add the peas, edamame and Swiss chard to the broth. Allow them to cook for 1 minute, then season carefully to taste. Divide the broth and vegetables into four bowls with the chicken pieces on top. Serve with the horseradish sauce on the side.

Moussaka

SERVES 4

125g dried soya mince
4 tbsp olive oil
1 onion, chopped
3 cloves garlic, chopped
150ml red wine
1 tbsp tomato purée
2 x 400g tins chopped
   tomatoes
1 tsp dried oregano
1 tsp ground allspice
1 cinnamon stick
Pinch cumin seeds
3 aubergines, sliced
Salt and freshly ground
   black pepper

For the white sauce
75g stanol spread
75g plain flour
600ml unsweetened
   soya milk
1 egg yolk
60g Parmesan, grated
Pinch ground nutmeg

Traditionally made with lamb mince, this version uses soya mince as a healthy alternative. It freezes well too.

Put the soya mince in a bowl and pour over 375ml of boiling water. Leave to soak for about 30 minutes until the water has been absorbed.

Heat half the oil in a large saucepan, add the onion and garlic and cook gently until the onion has softened, about 5–10 minutes. Add the soya mince to the pan and cook until the mince is soft and cooked through, about 5 minutes.

Add the wine, tomato purée, chopped tomatoes, oregano, allspice, cinnamon stick and cumin seeds. Simmer, covered, for 30 minutes, stirring occasionally. Remove the cinnamon stick and season to taste.

Heat the remaining oil in a frying pan over a medium heat and fry the aubergine slices in batches until golden on both sides. Remove from the pan and drain on kitchen paper; season well with salt and pepper.

Preheat the oven to 190°C/375°F/Gas mark 5. To make the white sauce, melt the spread in a saucepan. Add the flour and cook for 30 seconds, stirring until the mixture forms a smooth paste. Gradually stir in the milk and bring to the boil. Whisk continuously and leave to simmer 10 minutes. Remove from the heat and stir in the egg yolk, Parmesan and nutmeg.

Place a layer of aubergine in the bottom of an oiled ovenproof dish, followed by half the mince mixture. Repeat and finish with a final layer of aubergine and white sauce. Season with pepper. Bake in the oven for 25–30 minutes, until the top is golden.

Beef and Jerusalem artichoke casserole

SERVES 4

2 tbsp plain flour
900g lean stewing steak,
   cut into 2cm cubes
2 tbsp olive oil
Handful fresh sage
500ml red wine
300ml beef stock
2 tbsp tomato purée
6 shallots, quartered
2 potatoes, peeled and
   cut into chunks
3 large carrots, cut
   into chunks
5 Jerusalem artichokes,
   peeled and cut into chunks
2 parsnips, diced
1 sweet potato, peeled and
   cut into chunks
400g tin black-eyed beans,
   rinsed and drained
Salt and freshly ground
   black pepper

Eaten a couple of times a week, red meat can be part of a healthy balanced diet, especially when offset by a good dose of fibre, as in this hearty stew. Jerusalem artichokes contain probiotics that feed the good bacteria in the digestive system.

Preheat the oven to 150°C/300°F/Gas mark 2.

Mix the flour with some salt and pepper in a bowl. Toss the diced beef in the seasoned flour and set aside. Heat the olive oil in a large ovenproof pan over a medium heat. Add the beef in batches and sear on all sides; remove from the pan with a slotted spoon while you cook the rest.

Return all the browned beef to the pan and add the sage, red wine, stock and tomato purée. Cover with a lid or foil and place in the oven. After 1½ hours add the shallots, root vegetables and beans and return to the oven for a further 1½ hours.

After 3 hours of cooking the liquid should have reduced and thickened; if there is still too much liquid, remove the lid and return to the oven for another 30 minutes.

Half and half chilli

SERVES 8

125g dried soya mince
3 tbsp rapeseed oil
500g beef mince
2 onions, finely chopped
2 sticks celery, chopped
1 tsp chipotle paste
1 tbsp dried chilli flakes
Pinch cayenne pepper
2 cloves
1 tbsp finely chopped
    fresh oregano
2 x 400g tins chopped
    tomatoes
1 tbsp tomato purée
500ml beef stock
400g tin kidney beans,
    rinsed and drained
400g tin black-eyed beans,
    rinsed and drained
75g plain chocolate
    (minimum 70% cocoa
    solids), broken into pieces
Handful fresh coriander,
    roughly chopped
250g unsweetened soya
    yoghurt, to serve
Steamed brown basmati
    rice, to serve
Salt and freshly ground
    black pepper

Chilli is a great dish to make when feeding a crowd as it can be prepared in advance and then left to simmer away. Adding dried chilli flakes gives it an extra spicy kick and the chocolate provides a lovely richness.

Preheat the oven to 150°C/300°F/Gas mark 2. Put the soya mince into a bowl and pour over 375ml of boiling water. Leave to soak for about 30 minutes until the water has been absorbed.

Heat 2 tablespoons of the oil in a large ovenproof pan over a medium-high heat. Add the beef mince and fry until browned all over. Remove from the pan with a slotted spoon and set aside.

Add the remaining oil to the pan and fry the onions and celery for 3–4 minutes until the onions are soft, but not coloured. Stir in the chipotle paste, chilli flakes, cayenne pepper, cloves and oregano and cook for a further 2 minutes. Add the soya mince and cook for 2 minutes.

Return the beef mince to the pan, then stir in the chopped tomatoes, tomato purée, stock, and beans. Bring to the boil, then reduce the heat and cover with a tight-fitting lid. Place in the preheated oven and cook for 2–3 hours.

Remove from the oven and taste and adjust the seasoning. Stir in the chocolate pieces until they have just melted, then scatter over most of the chopped coriander.

Serve the chilli with soya yoghurt and brown basmati rice. Garnish with the remaining chopped coriander.

Cottage pie with butter bean and celeriac topping

SERVES 4

62g dried soya mince
2 tbsp olive oil
250g beef mince
1 large onion, diced
2 sticks celery, diced
2 carrots, diced
400g tin chopped tomatoes
2 tbsp tomato purée
1 tbsp Worcestershire sauce
1 bay leaf
1 tsp fresh thyme leaves,
    chopped
300ml beef or vegetable stock
Salt and freshly ground
    black pepper

For the topping
500g celeriac, peeled
    and cubed
400g tin butter beans,
    rinsed and drained
100g unsweetened
    soya yoghurt
4 tbsp stanol spread
2 leeks, trimmed and
    cut into 3mm slices
Salt and freshly ground
    black pepper

Combining lean minced beef with soya mince and topping it with butter beans means that you get all the flavour of a familiar cottage pie, while helping to reduce cholesterol at the same time.

Put the soya mince into a bowl and pour over 190ml of boiling water. Leave to soak for about 30 minutes until the water has been absorbed.

Heat the oil in a large saucepan, add the beef mince and brown on all sides. Stir in the soya mince and cook for another minute. Add the onion, celery and carrots and cook for about 10 minutes, until softened.

Stir in the chopped tomatoes, tomato purée, Worcestershire sauce, bay leaf, thyme leaves and stock. Add salt and pepper and bring to the boil. Cover and simmer for about 30 minutes, stirring occasionally.

Preheat the oven to 200°C/400°F/Gas mark 6.

To make the topping, bring a large saucepan of water to the boil and cook the celeriac until soft, about 18–20 minutes. Drain well and return to the pan. Add the butter beans and soya yoghurt along with a tablespoon of the spread and mash until smooth.

Heat the remaining spread in a pan and gently sauté the leeks over a medium heat. Add them to the celeriac and bean mash and season well to taste. Pour the cooked mince mixture into an ovenproof dish and top with mash. Bake in the oven for 20–30 minutes, until the top is golden brown and the filling is hot.

Herb-crusted lamb with white bean purée

SERVES 4

9 tbsp olive oil, plus
  extra for drizzling
2 x 8-bone racks
  of lamb, well trimmed
  (ask your butcher)
2 tbsp Dijon mustard
400g tin butter beans,
  rinsed and drained
1 clove garlic, chopped
6 anchovy fillets
1 sprig fresh rosemary,
  leaves chopped
Juice of ½ lemon
250g spinach leaves
Salt and freshly ground
  black pepper

For the herb crust
50g fresh wholemeal
  breadcrumbs
2 tbsp flat-leaf parsley,
  roughly chopped
2 tbsp thyme leaves
2 tbsp fresh rosemary
  leaves
Zest of 1 lemon
25g grated Parmesan
1 tbsp olive oil

This is a fantastic way to jazz up a simple lamb rack. The garlic and Parmesan crust is simply delicious.

Preheat the oven to 200°C/400°F/Gas mark 6.

Tip the ingredients for the herb crust into a food processor and whizz until well combined. Set aside.

Heat 1 tablespoon of the olive oil in an ovenproof frying pan. Season the lamb, then add to the pan and brown well on all sides. Turn off the heat. Turn the racks so that they are fat-side up, and brush liberally with the mustard. Press the herb crust all over the lamb and drizzle with a little olive oil; keep any leftover herb crust to one side.

Place the pan in the preheated oven and roast for 25 minutes until the crust is golden and the lamb is cooked – it should be pink in the middle but cooked all the way through. For rare lamb, reduce the cooking time to 20 minutes; or for well done, cook for 5 minutes more. Place the lamb on a board to rest.

Meanwhile, put the beans, garlic, anchovies, rosemary, lemon juice and salt and pepper in a food processor and whizz. Add enough oil to make a smooth purée. Tip the purée into a saucepan and place over a low heat to warm through.

Heat any remaining olive oil in a separate saucepan and add the spinach leaves; cook for 3 minutes until the leaves are just wilted.

To serve, carve the lamb into chops and divide the warm bean purée and spinach between serving plates. Sprinkle over any reserved herb crust.

Lamb tagine

SERVES 4

2 tbsp rapeseed oil
1 large onion, finely chopped
2 cloves garlic, crushed
2 tsp ground coriander
1 tsp ground cumin
1 tsp ground cinnamon
1 tsp smoked paprika
Pinch ground nutmeg
400g boneless lamb from
   the leg, trimmed and
   cut into 2cm cubes
400g tin chopped tomatoes
500ml lamb or beef stock
200g pumpkin, peeled
   and cubed
400g tin chickpeas, rinsed
   and drained
200g dried apricots
120g blanched almonds
Grated zest of 1 lemon
Small bunch fresh coriander,
   roughly chopped
Salt and freshly ground
   black pepper
Brown basmati rice, to serve

As with other red meat, lamb can still be enjoyed occasionally, especially when combined with one or more of the six cholesterol-lowering foods. Here the chickpeas add fibre while the almonds count as a healthy dose of nuts.

Preheat the oven to 200°C/400°F/Gas mark 6. Heat the rapeseed oil in a large, lidded ovenproof pan over a medium heat. Add the onion and cook for 5 minutes until softened but not coloured. Add the garlic and ground spices and cook, stirring, for 1–2 minutes.

Add the cubed lamb to the pan and then pour over the tomatoes and stock. Season with salt and pepper and bring to the boil. Cover and cook in the preheated oven for 1 hour. Remove the tagine and reduce the oven temperature to 150°C/300°F/Gas mark 2. Add the pumpkin, chickpeas and apricots, give the tagine a gentle stir and return to the oven, uncovered, for a further 30–40 minutes, until the pumpkin is tender.

Taste and adjust the seasoning. Stir in the almonds and then sprinkle over the lemon zest and chopped coriander. Serve in deep bowls with brown rice.

SWEET
TREATS

Strawberry frozen yoghurt

SERVES 4

4 over-ripe bananas
150g strawberries, hulled
500g unsweetened
   soya yoghurt
120g shelled pistachios,
   roughly chopped

Frozen yoghurt is a really good healthy alternative to ice cream and adding nuts makes it even more beneficial when it comes to managing cholesterol. This is also a fantastic dessert to prepare in advance.

Peel the bananas and cut them into chunks. Place on a tray lined with non-stick baking parchment, cover with cling film and place in the freezer overnight.

The next day, place the frozen bananas in a food processor and whizz until smooth, stopping occasionally to scrape down the sides of the bowl. Add half the strawberries to the bananas and whizz again. Roughly chop the remaining strawberries and set aside.

Pour the banana mixture into a large bowl and stir in the yoghurt. Finally, fold in the reserved chopped strawberries and pistachios.

Transfer the mixture to a lidded plastic container and place in the freezer overnight. Remove from the freezer about 10 minutes before serving to allow the frozen yoghurt to soften slightly. This will keep in the freezer for up to a month.

Nectarines with pistachio crumble

SERVES 4

200g jumbo oats
120g shelled pistachios
½ tsp ground cinnamon
2 tbsp clear honey
1 tbsp rapeseed oil
6 ripe nectarines,
   halved and stoned
50g golden caster sugar
2 star anise
Zest and juice of 1 orange
8 tbsp unsweetened soya
   yoghurt, to serve

A healthier take on the traditional fruit crumble, this pudding combines the sweetness of cooked fruit with the cholesterol-lowering benefits of oats and nuts. Any fruit or combination of fruit would work – try it with fresh figs.

Preheat the oven to 200°C/400°F/Gas mark 6. Combine the oats, pistachios and cinnamon in a large bowl and add the honey and oil; stir until well combined. Tip on to a non-stick baking sheet and spread out evenly. Bake in the oven for 15–20 minutes, stirring halfway through cooking to prevent the edges burning. Remove from the oven when the mixture is crisp and golden brown and set aside to cool.

Place the halved nectarines in a large pan with the sugar, star anise and orange zest and juice. Cook over a high heat for 3–4 minutes until the sugar has dissolved, then reduce the heat, cover and simmer for a further 7–10 minutes, or until the fruit has softened but still retains its shape. Remove the star anise and discard.

Divide the cooked fruit between warmed serving bowls, spoon the oat and nut crunch over the top and serve immediately with a few dollops of yoghurt.

Spiced poached pears

SERVES 4

1 tbsp clear honey
1 tbsp redcurrant or
   cranberry jelly
1 cinnamon stick
½ tsp mixed spice
2 spiced fruit tea bags, such
   as apple and cinnamon
4 firm pears, peeled, halved
   and cored
Handful fresh cranberries
8 tbsp unsweetened
   soya yoghurt
60g shelled pistachios,
   roughly chopped

A very autumnal dessert that is low in sugar. Chopped nuts add a good crunchy texture, which works well with the soft fruit.

Put the honey, jelly, spices and tea bags into a large, lidded saucepan with 600ml water and bring to the boil. Add the pear halves, then cover and reduce the heat. Simmer for about 15 minutes until the pears are just tender.

Lift out the pears and transfer to a serving bowl. Return the pan to the heat and boil for 2–3 minutes before adding the cranberries. Continue to bubble for 3–5 minutes until the cranberries soften and the liquid turns syrupy. Remove and discard the tea bags and allow to cool slightly. Pour the syrup over the pears.

Combine the yoghurt and pistachios, reserving a few nuts for decoration. Serve the pears warm with a generous dollop of the yoghurt and a few extra pistachios sprinkled on the top.

Lime yoghurt crunch

SERVES 4

60g shelled pistachios
500g unsweetened
  soya yoghurt
Grated zest of 2 limes

For the granola
250g jumbo oats
100g walnuts, roughly
  chopped
1 tbsp wheatgerm
2 tbsp olive oil
1 tsp clear honey
½ tsp ground cinnamon
1 large egg white

A great-tasting dessert that is practically sugar-free is quite hard to come by so this is a popular choice for those looking for a heart-healthy alternative.

Blitz the pistachios in a food processor until you have rough crumbs.

Preheat the oven to 150°C/300°F/Gas mark 2 and line a baking sheet with non-stick baking parchment. Make the granola by combining the oats, walnuts, wheatgerm, olive oil, honey and cinnamon in a large bowl, tossing to coat evenly.

In a separate bowl, whisk the egg white until white and frothy. Stir into the granola mixture, distributing it evenly throughout. Spread the mixture in a single layer on the lined baking sheet. Bake in the oven for 50 minutes. About halfway through the cooking time, use a large spatula to turn over sections of the granola carefully. When it is evenly browned and feels dry to the touch, transfer to a cooling rack. Allow to cool completely before breaking up into clusters.

Stir the lime zest into the soya yoghurt.

Place a layer of granola clusters in the bottom of four glasses or bowls. Top with a generous tablespoon of the lime yoghurt and a generous amount of chopped pistachios. Repeat this layering process and serve immediately.

Apple, apricot and almond strudel

SERVES 6

2 dessert apples, peeled,
  cored and grated
200g tinned apricots
  in juice, drained and
  roughly chopped
180g ground almonds
Few drops almond extract
1–2 tsp clear honey
6 filo pastry sheets,
  about 30 x 20cm
6 tbsp olive oil
20g sesame seeds (optional)

This simple strudel combines the natural sweetness of apples and apricots with honey and ground almonds to give a dessert that is warming and filling yet still low in sugar.

Preheat the oven to 180°C/350°F/Gas mark 4 and line a baking sheet with non-stick baking parchment.

Place the grated apple, chopped apricots, ground almonds, almond extract and honey in a large bowl and stir together until well combined. Set aside.

Take a sheet of filo pastry and brush with plenty of olive oil. Place the next sheet on top and brush with oil again; repeat with all six sheets. Spread the fruit and almond mixture over the top of the pastry sheets in an even layer, leaving about 2cm uncovered along one long end. Starting at the other long end, roll up the pastry and then carefully transfer to your lined baking sheet.

Brush the top of the strudel with some olive oil and if using, sprinkle over the sesame seeds. Bake in the oven for 30–40 minutes until the pastry is crisp and golden brown.

Chocolate and butter bean brownie

MAKES 12

400g tin butter beans,
   rinsed and drained
2–3 stanol shots
250g apple sauce
200g self-raising flour
2 tsp baking powder
Pinch salt
3 tbsp cocoa powder
3 eggs
50g caster sugar
Few drops vanilla extract
180g pecan nuts,
   roughly chopped

Butter beans might not be the first thing you think of for a brownie but the addition of beans provides a lovely moist texture. To get the dose stated on the left, you'll need to eat two brownies – we're pretty sure this won't be hard!

Preheat the oven to 180°C/350°F/Gas mark 4 and lightly grease a 30 x 20cm baking tray.

Place the beans and 2 stanol shots in a food processor and whizz together until smooth – you are looking for the consistency of mashed potato. Add more stanol shot if the mixture looks too dry. Add the apple sauce and process again for a minute or two, until smooth and well combined.

Sift the flour, baking powder, salt and cocoa powder into a large bowl. In a separate bowl, beat the eggs with an electric whisk and then add the sugar in 3 or 4 batches, beating well after each addition. Add one-third of the bean mixture to the egg mixture together with one-third of the flour mixture and fold in carefully. Repeat twice more until all the ingredients are gently incorporated.

Add the vanilla extract and pecan nuts and gently fold through. Pour the mixture into the baking tray and spread out evenly. Bake in the oven for 30–35 minutes – check to see if the brownie is done by inserting a skewer into the middle – it should come out almost clean. Allow to cool before cutting into squares. Keeps for a few days if stored in an airtight jar.

Florentines

MAKES 8

50g soya spread
1 tsp ground ginger
1 tbsp caster sugar
1 tbsp plain flour
100ml unsweetened
   soya yoghurt
50g flaked almonds
60g blanched almonds
60g brazil nuts, chopped
50g dried cranberries
50g dark chocolate
   (minimum 70% cocoa
   solids), broken into pieces

These florentines are not only surprisingly easy to make, but they are also low in sugar. Buy the best quality chocolate you can find with a high cocoa content.

Preheat the oven to 180°C/350°F/Gas mark 4. Put the soya spread, ginger, sugar and flour into a saucepan and heat over a medium heat, stirring continuously, until the sugar has dissolved and the ingredients are well combined. Add the soya yoghurt, a little at a time, again stirring continuously. Add the almonds, brazil nuts, cranberries and mix well until combined.

Line a baking sheet with non-stick baking parchment and place teaspoonfuls of the florentine mixture on to it, making sure they are well spaced.

Bake in the oven for 15 minutes, or until golden brown. Remove from the oven and carefully transfer them to a cooling rack with a spatula.

While the florentines are cooling, bring a small saucepan of water to a gentle simmer and place a heatproof bowl on top, making sure the base of the bowl does not touch the water. Add the chocolate pieces and stir until smooth and melted.

Turn the florentines over so that the flat base is facing upwards. Use a spoon to drizzle the melted chocolate over the florentine bases in zig-zag patterns and set aside to cool and set. Keeps for a few days if stored in an airtight container.

Almond and cranberry cake

SERVES 8

100g soya spread
60g caster sugar
3 eggs, beaten
120g ground almonds
120g plain flour
2 tsp baking powder
100g fresh cranberries,
    chopped
200g blanched whole
    almonds, roughly chopped
50g flaked almonds
Icing sugar, to dust (optional)

Cake and cholesterol don't usually go together but by adding almonds you can enjoy treats like this occasionally and still keep an eye on heart health.

Preheat the oven to 180°C/350°F/Gas mark 4 and grease and line a 20cm round springform cake tin.

Put the soya spread and sugar in a large bowl and beat together with an electric mixer until light and fluffy, scraping down the sides of the bowl as you go to make sure it is evenly mixed.

Gradually add the eggs to the mixture, beating well after each addition. Gently fold in the ground almonds with a metal spoon. Sift the flour and baking powder into the bowl and carefully fold in. Once all the flour is mixed in, fold in the cranberries and whole almonds, taking care not to overmix.

Pour the mixture into the prepared tin and spread evenly over the base. Scatter the flaked almonds over the top and bake in the oven for 40–45 minutes until the cake is golden brown and firm to the touch. To check for doneness, insert a skewer into the centre – if it comes out clean the cake is cooked. Allow to cool. If using, dust with icing sugar just before serving.

Oat and berry scones

MAKES 8

250g self-raising flour,
  plus extra for dusting
Pinch salt
50g golden caster sugar,
  plus extra for sprinkling
50g fine oatmeal
50g stanol spread, chilled
  and cut into small pieces
1 egg
3 stanol shots
100g raspberries
Milk, for brushing
Stanol spread or Almond
  Butter (page 29),
  to serve

These scones have a wonderful texture and colour too, thanks to the berries. They are good enough to eat on their own but are especially tasty spread with Almond Butter.

Preheat the oven to 220°C/425°F/Gas mark 7 and line a baking sheet with non-stick baking parchment.

Sift the flour, salt and sugar into a large bowl and then stir in the oatmeal. Add the spread and use your fingertips to work it into the dry ingredients until the mixture resembles fine breadcrumbs.

Beat the egg with the stanol shots and add to the bowl. Use a spatula to bring the mixture together into a soft dough. Gently fold in the raspberries until evenly distributed taking care not to squash them too much.

Dust your work surface with flour and turn out the dough. Gently pat down to a thickness of about 3cm and then use a cutter or knife to cut out 8 scones. Place on the baking sheet, brush the tops of each scone with milk and then sprinkle with a little sugar. Bake in the oven for 15 minutes until risen and golden. Serve warm with Almond Butter or spread.

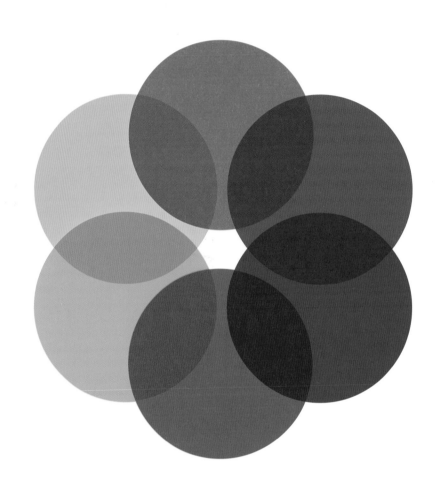

THE SIX FOODS DIET PLAN

Frequently asked questions

Cholesterol is a complex subject and a rapidly evolving area of medical science. In this section we look at some of those frequently asked questions and aim to give you clear answers. But if you have a burning question that we haven't covered, email us at health@mailonsunday.co.uk.

Q: *What exactly is cholesterol?*
A: Cholesterol is a waxy substance that has multiple beneficial roles in the body, from making hormones to aiding digestion. Generally less than 25 per cent of cholesterol comes from the diet, and the vast majority, certainly more than 75 per cent, is made by our own body, and mostly in the liver.

As it is a fatty substance, it won't mix with blood, which is largely water. So the body transports it wrapped in proteins, as tiny parcels called lipoproteins. There are two main types, HDL (high-density lipoprotein) and LDL (low-denstiy lipoprotein) cholesterol. LDL is the type that, if found in higher concentrations in the blood, can trigger processes that may lead to heart disease. People that do have high LDL cholesterol, along with other risk factors, may well be told by their doctor to reduce their levels. HDL, on the other hand protects against damage.

Q: *How is cholesterol measured?*
A: It can only be done via a blood test. You can't tell a person's cholesterol levels just by looking at them, which means that people are often surprised by the results. In the UK and Europe, cholesterol is measured in millimoles per litre of blood (mmol/l). However, in the USA a different scale is used – milligrams per decilitre (mg/dl). Most people simply know they have a number, as the whole mmol/l addition is unmemorable and clunky, and for simplicity we've just used a simple number too.

Q: *What is considered high cholesterol?*
A: In the UK we have very high levels of heart disease and the Department of Health recognises a total cholesterol level that is over 5.0 or an LDL cholesterol over 3.0 as high. The LDL level is not actually measured but calculated from the total and the HDL levels using a mathematical formula. So it is actually the ratio between total and HDL cholesterol that matters most. It can be easier to lower LDL than to raise HDL, and until recently most of the research into cholesterol levels has focused on LDL lowering. If you are at particular risk of heart disease due to other factors such as a family history of heart disease, if you are overweight, a smoker, or inactive for instance, or you already have heart problems, the recommended levels are a total cholesterol of less than 4.0 and an LDL of less than 2.0. Your HDL should be as high as possible, but at least above 1.0.

Q: Why is my cholesterol high?

A: A common cause is eating the wrong foods and lack of exercise. However, some people have high cholesterol levels even though they think that they have a healthy diet. There is strong scientific evidence that our genes play an important role in the natural variation of cholesterol levels between individuals, as well as how we respond to cholesterol in the diet. If you have a genetic tendency to run high levels then medication is probably essential. Equally some people have low levels no matter what they eat.

In more than 1 in 500 people in the UK, very high cholesterol runs in the family due to a genetic problem called familial hypercholesterolaemia. When someone has this faulty gene from a parent, cholesterol tends to be over 8.0 (or 6.0 in children) and there is a risk of heart attacks in their 40s. One in a million people have two copies of the gene. They can have cholesterol levels of 20.0 or more – and may have heart attacks even as teenagers.

Only rarely is a high cholesterol level due to another condition. Other causes include an underactive thyroid gland, obesity, drinking a lot of alcohol and some rare kidney and liver disorders.

Q: Does a high reading mean I'm going to have a heart attack?

A: No, it is just one of a number of risk factors. But a strong link between high cholesterol levels and the risk of heart disease has been shown in many scientific studies over the years. However, cholesterol levels vary widely and in fact, most people who have heart attacks will be within the top of the 'normal' range. So even normal may not be ideal for you. Your doctor will carry out a cardiac risk assessment, taking into account all the factors before deciding on a course of action. It is important to follow the advice of your doctor or health professional.

Q: Why do some people have heart attacks while others with similar cholesterol levels don't?

A: The underlying problem leading to heart attacks is a process called atherosclerosis – literally 'hardening of the arteries'. Most people imagine this as slow furring up of the arteries with fatty deposits, rather like a central heating system where the pipes get clogged up over the years. In fact atherosclerosis is rather more like a teenager getting spots, although in this case the spots are in the lining of your arteries rather than on the skin. These spots, or plaques, contain deposits of LDL that become oxidised in the artery wall, rather like butter going rancid, and therefore become highly toxic. This leads the plaques to become inflamed. Eventually, the inflammation dies down and leaves a scar in the wall, which calcifies, causing hardening of the normally elastic arteries. This can narrow the arteries and cause chest pain (angina), which is due to cramp in the heart muscle when you try to exercise.

More dangerously, when the plaques are soft, they can sometimes burst and split the lining of the artery. This triggers a blood clot inside the artery that can block the blood flow and cause sudden angina or even a heart attack.

Plaque formation and rupture on a minute level is happening frequently in many of us after the age of 40. We can't feel it happening and the plaques themselves don't generally narrow the arteries enough to restrict blood flow and cause pain.

The higher your LDL cholesterol level, the more plaques you tend to get. But the number of plaques – and, just as importantly, the risk of them bursting – also depends on other factors like your genes, smoking cigarettes, diabetes, high blood pressure, lack of exercise and of course, the food you eat.

Q: How long before you know how well the diet works?
A: Studies vary in length from one to three months or more, but if you adopt all the healthy eating recommendations we make you should really see the benefits within three months. If you don't get your levels down enough, speak to your doctor.

Q: What are statins, and how do they work?
A: Statins are a type of medicine that blocks one of the most important enzymes used by the body to make cholesterol. Statins also increase the LDL receptors on the liver cells, encouraging the liver to remove more LDL from circulation. With less cholesterol manufactured and more removed by the body the cholesterol level in the blood falls. What's more, the statins seem to have a powerful effect in reducing the inflammation in the artery plaques. These combined features may be why statins are so powerful in protecting from heart disease.

Q: How high does your cholesterol level need to be before you have to go on statins?
A: It doesn't have to be very high at all. In fact the benefit of statins is seen whatever level of cholesterol you run. It depends more on your risk of cardiovascular disease than on your cholesterol blood tests. At times, doctors will recommend statins to patients who have low levels of cholesterol, while other people with higher levels may not be at sufficiently high risk of atherosclerosis to benefit from them.

Q: *If I am already on statins, why do I need to watch what I eat?*
A: Statins are highly effective at lowering LDL cholesterol and reducing the risk of plaque rupture, but even powerful statins may not be enough to get your levels right down. What is more, they are not very good at raising your HDL cholesterol. Most people tolerate statins without any problems but higher doses do increase the risk of side effects.

For these reasons, a diet to improve your cholesterol will help. The right foods will offer some protection from heart disease and strokes whatever your cholesterol levels and the latest studies show they help even on top of medical treatment.

Q: *If I reduce my cholesterol level, does it mean I won't have a heart attack?*
A: There is no guarantee of this. However, it will tilt the odds firmly in your favour. It may not be enough if you continue, for example, to smoke. Smoking is perhaps one of the most significant risk factors in heart disease, so smoking will very probably override these dietary changes.

Q: *How often should I have a cholesterol test?*
A: If you have a family history of high cholesterol, strokes or heart attacks, you should have your cholesterol tested when you are young – at 20, or even younger, if your doctor is worried. Even if you don't have a family history, you should test your cholesterol at about 40 years of age, and then at least every five years, or more often if you are at risk or your levels are high. Your doctor will advise you on this.

Week 1 Meal planner

	Monday	Tuesday	Wednesday
Breakfast	Perfect granola (page 26)	Almond butter on toasted muffins (page 29)	Blueberry instant porridge with soya milk (page 28)
Lunch	Smoked mackerel salad (page 62)	Chicken and asparagus salad (page 66)	Avocado and bean wrap (page 56)
Snack/Pudding	Oat berry smoothie (page 26)	Oatcakes with beetroot hummus (page 72)	Oat berry smoothie (page 26)
Supper	Cottage pie with butter bean and celeriac topping (page 150)	Tuna steak with mango salsa and spicy bean cakes *plus one stanol shot (page 102)	Tomato and pesto filo pizza (page 126)

Thursday	Friday	Saturday	Sunday
Oat-crusted kippers with eggs, mushrooms and spinach (page 46)	**Kedgeree** (page 44)	**Apple juice bircher with yoghurt, cinnamon and walnuts** (page 35)	**French toast with plums** (page 30)
Spicy bean soup (page 90)	**Turkey pilaf** (page 138)	**Trout and horseradish pâté** (page 57)	**Mexican hash** (page 50)
Oatcakes with sardine pâté (page 81)	**Oatcakes with mashed bean dip** (page 81)	**Nectarines with pistachio crumble** (page 160)	**Oatcakes with spicy satay chicken** (page 80)
Pistachio chicken drumsticks (page 113)	**Herb-crusted lamb with white bean purée** *plus one stanol shot (page 152)	**Lemon prawns** (page 104)	**Broccoli and cashew nut stir-fry** *plus one stanol shot (page 88)

Week 2 Meal planner

	Monday	Tuesday	Wednesday
Breakfast	Apple juice bircher with mango and hazelnut crunch (page 35)	Eggs with spicy tomatoes and beans (page 40)	Blueberry instant porridge with soya milk (page 28)
Lunch	Chicken soba noodles (page 65)	Chickpea hazelnut, sweet potato and butternut squash salad (page 52)	Baked sweet potato with spicy chickpeas (page 55)
Snack/Pudding	Oat berry smoothie (page 26)	Oatcakes with spicy satay chicken (page 80)	Oat berry smoothie (page 26)
Supper	Crab and bean fishcakes (page 135)	Fish crumble (page 130)	Harissa chicken (page 116)

Thursday	Friday	Saturday	Sunday
Bircher with rhubarb and ginger compote (page 34)	**Oat berry smoothie** (page 26)	**Perfect granola** (page 26)	**Oat pancakes with bananas** (page 33)
Chicken, butter bean and walnut salad (page 68)	**Nut and bean tabbouleh** (page 60)	**Pulled pork with refried beans** (page 136)	**Curried chicken salad** (page 114)
Oat and berry scones (page 175)	**Minted pea and soya bean hummus (with oatcakes)** (page 73)	**Lime yoghurt crunch** (page 164)	**Macadamia nut hummus (with oatcakes)** (page 73)
Lamb tagine *plus one smart food shot (page 154)	**Fruity South African chicken** (page 111)	**Citrus salmon salad** (page 98) *plus one smart food shot	**Goat's cheese, asparagus and soya bean risotto** *plus one smart food shot (page 93)

Recipe index

Page 42
Chickpea and spinach frittata
● ◐ ○ ○ ○ ◐
544
calories per portion

Page 40
Eggs with spicy tomatoes and beans
● ◐ ○ ○ ○ ○
596
calories per portion

Page 93
Goat's cheese, asparagus and soya bean risotto
● ○ ● ○ ○ ○
213
calories per portion

Page 52
Chickpea, hazelnut, sweet potato and butternut salad
● ● ○ ◐ ○ ○
665
calories per portion

Page 58
Feta and pomegranate couscous with almonds
● ◐ ● ◐ ○ ○
703
calories per portion

Page 148
Half and half chilli
● ● ○ ○ ○ ○
325
calories per portion

Page 168
Chocolate and butter bean brownie
◐ ○ ○ ○ ○ ○
222
calories per portion

Page 108
Fish chowder
● ○ ● ○ ○ ○
277
calories per portion

Page 116
Harissa chicken
◐ ● ○ ○ ● ○
992
calories per portion

Page 98
Citrus salmon salad
● ○ ● ○ ○ ○
592
calories per portion

Page 130
Fish crumble
● ◐ ● ○ ○ ○
587
calories per portion

Page 152
Herb-crusted lamb with white bean puree
● ● ○ ○ ○ ○
812
calories per portion

Page 150
Cottage pie with butter bean and celeriac topping
● ○ ● ○ ○ ◐
402
calories per portion

Page 170
Florentines
● ◐ ● ○ ○ ○
349
calories per portion

Page 44
Kedgeree
● ● ○ ○ ○ ○
910
calories per portion

Page 135
Crab and bean fishcakes
● ● ○ ○ ○ ○
397
calories per portion

Page 30
French toast with plums
◐ ◐ ○ ○ ○ ○
240
calories per portion

Page 154
Lamb tagine
● ○ ○ ● ○ ○
644
calories per portion

Page 114
Curried chicken salad
● ○ ● ● ○ ○
641
calories per portion

Page 111
Fruity South African chicken
◐ ◐ ○ ● ○ ◐
725
calories per portion

Page 104
Lemon prawns
◐ ○ ○ ○ ○ ○
241
calories per portion

Page 164
Lime yoghurt crunch

762
calories per portion

Page 60
Nut and bean tabbouleh

416
calories per portion

Page 81
Oatcakes with mashed bean dip

498
calories per portion

Page 73
Macadamia nut hummus

633
calories per portion

Page 175
Oat and berry scones

617
calories per portion

Page 81
Oatcakes with sardine pâté

396
calories per portion

Page 50
Mexican hash

500
calories per portion

Page 39
Oat beetroot muffins

193
calories per portion

Page 76
Olive bread sticks

571
calories per portion

Page 73
Minted pea and soya bean hummus

136
calories per portion

Page 26
Oat berry smoothie

246
calories per portion

Page 26
Perfect granola

512
calories per portion

Page 144
Moussaka

828
calories per portion

Page 33
Oat pancakes with bananas

331
calories per portion

Page 113
Pistachio chicken drumsticks

230
calories per portion

Page 94
Mushroom and quinoa risotto

598
calories per portion

Page 46
Oat-crusted kippers with eggs, mushrooms and spinach

566
calories per portion

Page 142
Poached chicken and spring vegetables

123
calories per portion

Page 160
Nectarines with pistachio crumble

471
calories per portion

Page 80
Oatcakes with spicy satay chicken

961
calories per portion

Page 121
Pork and apple meatballs

322
calories per portion

Page 136
Pulled pork with refried beans

414
calories per portion

Page 90
Spicy bean soup

200
calories per portion

Page 124
Tomato and spinach macaroni cheese

450
calories per portion

Page 84
Red pepper and goat's cheese muffins

213
calories per portion

Page 96
Spinach and chickpea gratin

531
calories per portion

Page 57
Trout and horseradish pâté

197
calories per portion

Page 77
Roasted seeds and soya beans

146
calories per portion

Page 128
Spinach, ricotta and cashew nut lasagne

931
calories per portion

Page 120
Turkey burgers

388
calories per portion

Page 106
Salmon and broccoli penne

363
calories per portion

Page 24
Yoghurt with almonds, honey and watermelon

390
calories per portion

Page 138
Turkey pilaf

738
calories per portion

Page 132
Sardine pasta bake

541
calories per portion

Page 158
Strawberry frozen yoghurt

267
calories per portion

Page 102
Tuna steak with mango salsa and spicy bean cakes

1015
calories per portion

Page 62
Smoked mackerel salad

847
calories per portion

Page 101
Thai tofu and rice noodle soup

442
calories per portion

Page 162
Spiced poached pears

448
calories per portion

Page 126
Tomato and pesto filo pizza

687
calories per portion

Index

fish 19
   haddock, smoked 130
   kippers 46
   mackerel, smoked 44, 62
   salmon 98, 108, 130
   salmon, smoked 106
   sardines in oil 81, 132
   trout 57
   tuna 102
   white fish 108

h
haddock, smoked 130
haricot beans 40, 60, 120
hazelnuts 35, 52, 96, 138
heart disease 7, 178, 179–180, 181
high-density lipoprotein (HDL) 8, 12, 14, 15
hyper-responders 18–19

j
Jerusalem artichokes 146

k
kidney beans 90, 102, 136, 148
kippers 46

l
lamb 18, 152, 154
lentils 118
limes 164
lipoproteins 7–8, 9, 12, 14, 15, 178
low-density lipoprotein (LDL) 8, 9, 15, 178

m
macadamia nuts 73
mangos 35, 102
muffins 39, 84
mushrooms 15, 46, 94, 132

n
nectarines 160
noodles 65, 101
nuts 8, 14
   almonds 14, 24, 26, 28, 29, 58, 154, 166, 170, 173
   almonds, ground 141, 166, 173
   Brazil nuts 14, 170
   cashew nuts 14, 65, 88, 98, 111, 128, 141
   hazelnuts 35, 52, 96, 138
   macadamia nuts 73
   peanut butter 80
   pecans 33, 168
   pine nuts 46, 66, 116, 126
   pistachios 113, 158, 160, 162, 164
   walnuts 35, 39, 60, 62, 68, 79, 114, 164

o
oats 8, 11, 15
   breakfast/brunch 26, 28, 33, 34, 35, 39, 46
   family meals 130
   snacks 80, 81
   sweet treats 160, 164, 175

oils 8, 12, 17: *see also* olive oil; rapeseed oil
olive oil 8, 12, 17
   breakfast/brunch 40, 42, 44, 46
   family meals 126, 132, 135, 136, 138, 144, 146, 150, 152
   lunch 52, 58, 60, 62, 65, 66, 68
   snacks 72, 73, 76, 77, 84
   suppers 90, 94, 96, 102, 104, 108, 111, 116, 121
   sweet treats 164, 166
olives 58, 76
orange juice 30, 34, 62, 160
oranges 62

p
pancakes 33
pasta 106, 124, 128, 132
pâtés 57, 81
peanut butter 80
pears 162
peas 73, 142
pecan nuts 33, 168
peppers, red and green 40, 42, 66, 84, 90, 111, 126, 132
pesto 126
pine nuts 46, 66, 116, 126
pinto beans 136
pistachios 113, 158, 160, 162, 164
pizza 126
plums 30
pomegranate 58